PRACTICE FOR U.S. CITIZENSHIP

Carlos F. Paz

68737

AN ARCO BOOK
Published by Prentice Hall Press
New York, NY 10023

First Edition, Fourth Printing, 1986

An Arco Book
Published by Prentice Hall Press
A Division of Simon & Schuster, Inc.
Gulf + Western Building
One Gulf + Western Plaza
New York, NY 10023

Library of Congress Cataloging in Publication Data

Paz, Carlos F.
  Practice for U.S. citizenship.

  1. Citizenship—United States.   2. United States—
Politics and government.   I. Title.
JK1758.P39   323.6′23′0973   81-10884
ISBN 0-668-05305-4   AACR2

Printed in the United States of America

Contents

Preface

What this book is all about:

In brief and simple language this book presents the requirements for naturalization, a short history of the United States and its government, and examples of the kinds of questions you will be asked in the written and oral examinations. The information provided here is not meant to take the place of the United States Immigration and Naturalization Service pamphlets, but simply to give additional help to the men and women who wish to become United States citizens.

    This book includes the basic facts, laws, and regulations you need to know to become a citizen, plus over 200 sample questions of the sort used by examiners.

Carlos F. Paz

How to Apply for Naturalization

If you are applying for citizenship, you will be tested on your knowledge of the government of the United States and its history. You will also be tested on your ability to read, write, and speak English, unless you have been living in the United States for a total of at least 20 years and were over 50 years old as of December 24, 1952, or unless you are physically unable to read, write, or speak.

GENERAL NATURALIZATION REQUIREMENTS

Every applicant must meet every requirement for naturalization, unless he or she is a person who comes within a special class that is exempt from some of those requirements. Check with the nearest office of the Immigration and Naturalization Service in your area to find which class you belong to.

FILING THE APPLICATION

The first step is to get an application form and, except for children under 14 years of age, a fingerprint card and a biographic information form from the nearest office of the Immigration and Naturalization Service. You can call by telephone and receive these papers by mail.

If you are applying for your own naturalization, the application form to be used is Form N-400, "Application to File Petition for Naturalization." If, however, a parent wants to file a petition for the naturalization of a child or an adopted child, the application to be used is Form N-402, "Application to File Petition of Naturalization in Behalf of Child."

The application, the fingerprint card, and the biographic information forms are furnished without charge. They must be filled out according to the instructions printed on them, and taken or mailed to the nearest office of Immigration and Naturalization Service. Along with the forms you must submit three photographs as described in the application.

EXAMINATION OF THE APPLICATION

After processing the application, the Immigration and Naturalization Service will inform you they have arranged an appointment with an examiner to discuss your application. The examiner will help you file the legal papers—known as "Petition for Naturalization"—in the Naturalization Court.

FINAL COURT HEARING

After the examination has been completed and the petition has been filed, you must wait for at least 30 days before you can have a final hearing in the Naturalization Court. Often the judge does not ask questions. However, it is wise to be on the safe side and be prepared to answer the questions you have been told you will be asked. When no questions are asked, the Naturalization Examiner informs the judge that you have been found qualified for naturalization and should be made a citizen.

When the court decides that you are eligible to become a citizen, you must take an Oath of Allegiance to the United States. In doing so, you give up allegiance to your former country and promise to support and defend the Constitution and laws of the United States.

SOME ADVICE TO REMEMBER WHEN YOU COME BEFORE THE EXAMINER OR COURT

Never be late for your appointment. If you are even a few minutes late for the examination of your application, you will be turned back, and a new date for the examination will be sent to you by mail.

If you are a man, wear a coat and tie; if you are a woman, wear a dress. DO NOT WEAR JEANS! Dress up for the occasion if you can.

Remember, always give your alien registration number when communicating with this service, and bring your card with you to the court hearing. You must turn it in to one of the examiners before you receive your Certificate of Naturalization. Lists of offices of the Immigration and Naturalization Service from which information may be obtained can be found in your local telephone directory under *United States Government*. If you cannot find the proper listing, dial Information.

History of the United States

Europeans came to America soon after its discovery. The Spanish began exploring Mexico, Central America, and parts of North America as early as 1510. Ponce de León landed on the east coast of Florida a few years later.

England sent a number of expeditions to explore the new world, largely on the east coast of North America. One man, Sir Walter Raleigh, led several expeditions and named the land he explored "Virginia," in honor of Elizabeth I, the Virgin Queen. But it was after the death of Elizabeth that a full-scale effort to establish English colonies in the New World began. This effort came from merchants—not from the new King, James I.

The first large group of settlers to leave England came here in 1620 for religious reasons. About 100 people set out from Plymouth, England, on a ship named the *Mayflower*. The ship landed in America on Cape Cod Bay. The settlers decided to remain, and claimed to be free of English law. Before going ashore, the Pilgrims drew up what they called the Mayflower Compact:

> We whose names are underwritten, do by these present, solemnly and mutually in the presence of God and one another covenant and combine ourselves under . . . into a civil body politic . . . and by virtue hereof do enact . . . such just and equal laws . . . as shall be thought must meet and convene for the general good of the colony.

This group of religious dissenters had, in their simple way, created a new government, with no laws controlling religious beliefs. In 1791 this declaration of freedom from religious persecution became part of the Constitution of the United States. English merchants continued to encourage emigration to the New World, and between 1660 and 1760 England had established 13 colonies in North America.

Settlers from other nations arrived—French, Irish, German, Dutch, and many others. With them came new cultures and life-styles. These people became the first Americans.

During this period of colonization, between 1660 and 1760, most colonists continued to look to England for leadership. The northern colonies (Pennsylvania, New York, and New England) became more commercially inclined, while the South remained agricultural. Farming was hard and expensive. This and other problems with white labor contributed to the shift toward the use of slaves. By 1740, there were about 150,000 slaves in the South.

Meanwhile, the thirteen colonies were growing and the people were, to a large extent, independent from the king. During this time, Europe was continually at war and many immigrants came here to avoid being drafted. But there was little fighting in the New World until 1752, when the French and English clashed. The governor of Virginia appointed a young man by the name of George Washington to the rank of Lieutenant Colonel, to fight the French. Peace came in 1763, and the French abandoned their claims to North America except for two small islands in the St. Lawrence River. Canada became another of England's possessions at this time.

Because of the need for more revenue, England now began to tighten its control in the colonies. The continued warring on the Continent as well as the war to drive the French out of America and Canada had been expensive, and the colonies were expected to help the economy by paying more taxes. Trouble broke out between the colonists and the British Army. Some Americans sought independence from England. In June 1774, Massachusetts called for the first meeting of delegates from the 13 colonies to take action. They agreed, and in September, the First Continental Congress met in Philadelphia, with only Georgia absent.

The Revolutionary War

In January 1775, England ordered armed troops to fire upon the citizens who were in revolt in Massachusetts. That incident is called "The Shot Heard Round the World." This armed action by England quickly rallied the other colonies to the cause of freedom. The American Revolution had begun.

The Continental Congress named George Washington, who had served as commander in chief of the Virginia militia, to command the Continental forces. On July 4, 1776, with the help of Thomas Jefferson, Benjamin Franklin, John Adams, Roger Sherman, and Robert Livingston, the new Congress adopted the Declaration of Independence. In March 1781, the Articles of Confederation had been ratified, and in 1783 the signing of the Treaty of Paris officially ended the seven-year American Revolutionary War. The new country had won its independence from England. General George Washington was a national hero; he is now called "The Father of our Country."

The new country struggled to establish a new government. England and Spain were still in control of the land beyond the 13 colonies, and the Indians threatened the peace. America was young and weak. The 13 states had problems with the economy; the national government was not able to pay its debts.

The founding fathers called for a convention to change the Articles of Confederation. They altered the loose confederation of the former 13 colonies into a federated form, with a national government holding many of the powers once controlled by the states. That required consent by all the states. The meeting took place in Philadelphia. Delaware ratified in December, 1787, North Carolina in November, 1789, and Rhode Island held out until May, 1790. The first election took place between January and February of 1789, with George Washington the unanimous choice as the first president of the United States. John Adams won the Vice-Presidency.

On April 30, 1789, Washington took the Oath of Office. The problems with France, England, and Spain continued until 1794. Finally, on June 24, 1795, George Washington submitted to the senate a treaty with England, worked out by Chief Justice John Jay. It is called Jay's Treaty. This improved relations with England and helped the new nation grow without fear of war.

Without this danger, the United States began to expand. The Mississippi was now opened and the West was also, with the Louisiana Purchase from France and the explorations of Lewis and Clark. Other explorations followed and brought back information about the size and resources of this new land. This was a period of expansion for the United States; unfortunately, wars with Indian tribes resulted. In 1812, war was again declared between the United States and England over freedom of the seas. The war was ended by the Treaty of Ghent in December 1814.

The country was again on the move towards prosperity, progress, and expansion. (See the chart of the Territorial Expansions.) By 1820 the country had achieved major economic growth. In March 1836 Texas declared its independence from Mexico. In April, Sam Houston attacked the Mexican Army (lead by General Santa Anna) and drove the Mexican Army out of Texas. He was elected President of the Republic of Texas. However, Texas was to join the United States after a short period of being a separate nation.

War between the United States and Mexico was declared in 1846. As a result of the conflict, Mexico lost part of California and New Mexico. With expansion, the question of slavery came up once again, North and South opposing each other on the issue.

As the United States grew larger and richer, the North became more industrialized, while the South remained almost totally agricultural. Because of this, the South needed cheap labor and continued to depend on slaves.

The Civil War

In the election of 1860, Abraham Lincoln became the 16th President of the United States. Slavery concerned Lincoln deeply. His election caused the South to threaten to secede from the Union. Shortly after Lincoln's election, the South and the North declared war upon each other; the Civil War began in 1861 and ended in 1865. Slavery was officially abolished in the Confederate States of America by the Emancipation Proclamation (Jan. 1, 1863).

The 11 Southern states were brought back into the Union. Americans now had to forget war and try to reunite the country.

By 1893 the United States had become an industrial giant.

Railroads, iron, oil, and electricity had changed the country into a great power and a world leader.

The Spanish-American War, 1898

Cuban rebels had been waging guerrilla warfare against Spain for many years. The United States wanted to oust the Spanish from Cuba, and in April 1898 Congress voted to recognize Cuba as an independent nation. American forces were sent to drive out the Spanish. Commodore George Dewey was ordered to move against the Spanish navy in the Philippine Islands (another Spanish possession); he defeated the Spanish fleet. Commodore Dewey asked for troops to be sent to hold Manila. In August, President William McKinley dispatched troops and Manila was captured. Meanwhile, Colonel Theodore Roosevelt was sent to Cuba; the Spanish surrendered on July 17. Puerto Rico and Guam, other Spanish possessions, became Territories of the United States. The Philippines were added, as well. In 1901, after a bitter fight between the United States and the Philippines, Congress allowed the islands to have their own civilian government. In July 1901 William Howard Taft became the first civilian Governor of the Philippines. In 1902 the United States pulled its troops out of Cuba, Puerto Rico, and Guam, but these countries remained United States Territories.

The Progressive Era

This period lasted from 1902 until America entered World War I. The Progressive Era was so called because of its relatively liberal outlook. The Seventeenth Amendment was adopted in 1913; this meant that United States Senators were no longer appointed but now elected by the people of each state.

Women were gaining support in their fight for the right to vote. However, this would not become a fact until 1920. The Anti-Trust Act was passed, making it illegal for large companies to band together and control one industry. Child labor laws were passed, and some protection was guaranteed workers in dangerous occupations. Public health became a legislative consideration, as well.

World War I—1914 to 1918

The United States had no wish to enter the war between Germany (and its allies) and France and Britain (and their allies). However, the sinking of the Lusitania in 1915 and the loss of freedom of the seas forced the United States into the war in 1917. Armistice was declared on November 11, 1918. The war had ended and the American people were ready to resume normal life.

Industrial output doubled from 1921 to 1929. But vast overextension of credit by the government and the public took its toll. On October 24, 1929, "Black Thursday", the stock market fell. This was the beginning of the Great Depression, which lasted from 1929 to 1939.

A New War Begins—World War II

When Germany invaded Poland in September 1939, Britain honored its treaty with Poland and declared war on Germany. There was little fighting during 1939. But in May of 1940, Germany altered events by first attacking Holland, Belgium, and Luxembourg, and then marching into France. In 1941 Germany invaded Russia. On December 7, 1941, the Japanese attacked Pearl Harbor, and war was declared on Japan and its allies by the United States. A peace treaty was signed in Europe in early 1945, but the war continued in the Pacific until the United States dropped its atom bomb on Hiroshima. Three days later, a second bomb hit Nagasaki. The Japanese surrendered on August 15, 1945. Following the end of World War II, the United States began, once again, to shift the economy from wartime back to peacetime.

Relations with America's former ally, Russia, gradually became strained. Historians call this unfriendly state of affairs the Cold War, due largely to Russia's and America's attempts to exert influence in the same areas. The economy thrived, unemployment was low, and business was booming. This boom in the economy and new peace was shattered in 1950 when North Koreans rumbled across the 38th parallel, which divided North and South Korea. American and United Nations troops fought the North Koreans until 1953. American troops remain in South Korea to this date.

Dwight D. Eisenhower became President in 1953. The economy was prosperous during the eight years Eisenhower was in office. One of the issues during his administration was Civil Rights; segregation in the Armed Forces was abolished at this time. But it was not until the Kennedy administration that stricter enforcement of Civil Rights became effective.

By August 1964, the United States was once again at war. In the early years of the Vietnamese War (from 1965 to 1967), about 165,000 American troops were fighting the Communists. By 1968, over 600,000 Americans were fighting. The war ended in January 1973. President Richard M. Nixon took credit for having ended the war.

The Nixon administration is a dark page in the history of the United States. During the investigation of the Watergate scandals, many officials called for his impeachment and resignation. His Vice President, Spiro T. Agnew, was accused of having accepted bribes when he was previously Governor of Maryland. Agnew resigned as Vice President and Nixon appointed Gerald R. Ford as Vice President, under the authority of the 25th Amendment. Meanwhile, the Watergate investigation continued. On August 8, 1974, Nixon announced his resignation. The next day, on August 9, 1974, Gerald Ford became the 38th President of the United States.

America in the 1980s is faced with many problems, but it is hoped that American technology, know-how, and determination will see a new beginning of the American dream.

(Note: The reader must remember that this short history is designed to meet the requirements for persons seeking to pass the necessary tests to become naturalized citizens of the United States. It is not meant to replace textbooks used in school.)

United States Government

Federal, State, and Local

The Constitution of the United States is called the "highest law of the land." It gives power to the Federal and State governments, and protects the rights of citizens. There are three branches to the Federal government: executive, judicial, and legislative.

Like the Federal government, each State has three branches: executive, judicial, and legislative. However, the governmental systems of the individual states are not all the same, because each state has its own constitution.

In state government the Governor, Lieutenant Governor, Secretary of State, Attorney General, and other officials are the executive branch. The Governor, like the President, has his duties which are spelled out in each state constitution.

The judicial system is unique in every state. Most, however, have a Supreme Court and a Court of Criminal Appeals. Their decisions can be overruled by the Federal courts and the United States Supreme Court.

The legislative branch of government in a state may also be unique with regard to structure, size, and power. The laws are created by the State Legislature, but when doubts arise about a new law or the authority of the state's local government, the courts decide whether they conflict with the United States Constitution. State legislators deal mostly with local matters affecting the cities.

A Mayor and a City Council are found in most cities. The City Council is a single chamber and its size can vary. Some City Councils have two members, others have as many as 50 or more. They are elected by popular vote.

American History

Questions and Answers

1. *Q.* Name the 13 original colonies.
   A.   1. Connecticut
       2. Delaware
       3. Georgia
       4. Maryland
       5. Massachusetts
       6. New Hampshire
       7. New Jersey
       8. New York
       9. North Carolina
      10. Pennsylvania
      11. Rhode Island
      12. South Carolina
      13. Virginia

2. *Q.* Who is called the "Father" of this country?
   A. George Washington.

3. *Q.* Who was the Commander-in-Chief of the American Army at the time of the Revolutionary War?
   A. George Washington.

4. *Q.* What do the stripes of the United States flag stand for?
   A. The original 13 states.

5. *Q.* What are the highest Mountains in the United States?
   A. The Rocky Mountains.

6. *Q.* Name the original 13 states.
   A.   1. Connecticut

2. Delaware
3. Georgia
4. Maryland
5. Massachusetts
6. New Hampshire
7. New Jersey
8. New York
9. North Carolina
10. Pennsylvania
11. Rhode Island
12. South Carolina
13. Virginia

7. *Q.* Who was George Washington?
   A. He was the Commander-in-Chief of the American Army at the time of the Revolutionary War. He was also the first President of the United States.

8. *Q.* Who was Abraham Lincoln?
   A. He was the 16th President of the United States. He freed the slaves and saved the Union.

9. *Q.* What is the Declaration of Independence?
   A. It is a document signed by the delegates from the 13 colonies on July 4, 1776, declaring that they were free and independent from Britain.

10. *Q.* What was the Revolutionary War?
    A. It was the war between the 13 colonies and Britain over taxes and freedom. The colonies won the war.

11. *Q.* When was the Revolutionary War?
    A. From 1775 to 1783.

12. *Q.* What was the Civil War?
    A. It was the war between the North and the South over slavery and economics. The North won the war.

13. *Q.* When was the Civil War?
    A. From 1861 to 1865.

14. *Q.* What do the stars of the United States flag represent?
    A. Each star represents a state.

15. *Q.* What is the name of the national anthem?
    A. *The Star Spangled Banner.*

16. *Q.* What are the most important documents in the history
        of the United States?
    A. 1. The Declaration of Independence.
        2. The Articles of Confederation.
        3. The Constitution.
        4. The Emancipation Proclamation.

17. *Q.* Who were the Pilgrims?
    A. They were among the first settlers to come to this coun-
        try seeking freedom of religion. They arrived in Mas-
        sachusetts in 1620.

18. *Q.* Who wrote the Constitution?
    A. Delegates from the 13 colonies.

19. *Q.* What is the United States?
    A. It is a federated union of 50 states.

20. *Q.* What is the capital of the United States?
    A. Washington, D.C.

21. *Q.* How many states are there in the United States?
    A. There are 50 states.

22. *Q.* Where does the President live?
    A. He lives in the White House in Washington, D.C.

23. *Q.* Who was the first President of the United States?
    A. George Washington.

24. *Q.* Who was the 16th President of the United States?
    A. Abraham Lincoln.

25. *Q.* What is the longest river in the United States?
    A. It is the Mississippi River.

26. *Q.* How many stars are there in the United States flag?
    A. There are 50 stars.

27. *Q.* How many stripes are there in the United States flag?
    A. There are 13 stripes (7 red and 6 white).

28. *Q.* What is the 4th of July?
    A. It is Independence Day of the United States.

29. *Q.* Have you studied the United States Constitution?
    A. Yes, I have.

30. *Q.* What is the Constitution?
    A. It is the highest law of the United States.

31. *Q.* Do you know the meaning of the colors of the United States flag?
    A. Yes: red is for courage, white is for purity, and blue is for justice and truth.

32. *Q.* Who wrote *The Star Spangled Banner?*
    A. It was written in 1814 by Francis Scott Key, a Maryland lawyer, during the bombardment of Fort McHenry. It was adopted by Congress as the national anthem in 1931.

33. *Q.* Name the territorial expansions.
    A. 1. Louisiana Purchase   1803
          2. Florida   1819
          3. Texas   1845
          4. Oregon   1846
          5. Mexican Cession   1848
          6. Gadsden Purchase   1853

7. Alaska	1867
8. Hawaii	1898
9. The Philippines	1898–1946
10. Puerto Rico	1898
11. Guam	1898
12. American Samoa	1900
13. Canal Zone	1904–1979
14. U.S. Virgin Islands	1917
15. Pacific Islands	1947
16. Trust Territory	1947

34. *Q.* Name the Presidents of the United States and give the years they were in office.

A.	
George Washington	1789–1797
John Adams	1797–1801
Thomas Jefferson	1801–1809
James Madison	1809–1817
James Monroe	1817–1825
John Quincy Adams	1825–1829
Andrew Jackson	1829–1837
Martin Van Buren	1837–1841
William Henry Harrison	1841
John Tyler	1841–1845
James Knox Polk	1845–1849
Zachary Taylor	1849–1850
Millard Fillmore	1850–1853
Franklin Pierce	1853–1857
James Buchanan	1857–1861
Abraham Lincoln	1861–1865
Andrew Johnson	1865–1869
Ulysses Simpson Grant	1869–1877
Rutherford Birchard Hayes	1877–1881
James Abram Garfield	1881
Chester Alan Arthur	1881–1885
Grover Cleveland	1885–1889
Benjamin Harrison	1889–1893
Grover Cleveland	1893–1897
William McKinley	1897–1901

Theodore Roosevelt	1901–1909
William Howard Taft	1909–1913
Woodrow Wilson	1913–1921
Warren Gamaliel Harding	1921–1923
Calvin Coolidge	1923–1929
Herbert Clark Hoover	1929–1933
Franklin Delano Roosevelt	1933–1945
Harry S. Truman	1945–1953
Dwight David Eisenhower	1953–1961
John Fitzgerald Kennedy	1961–1963
Lyndon Baines Johnson	1963–1969
Richard Milhous Nixon	1969–1974
Gerald Rudolph Ford (appointed)	1974–1977
James Earl Carter	1977–1981
Ronald Wilson Reagan	1981–

American Government

Questions and Answers

1. *Q.* How does the Government get the money needed to carry on its affairs?
   A. By taxation.

2. *Q.* Who levies the taxes?
   A. Congress.

3. *Q.* Where is the original document of the Constitution located?
   A. In the National Archives, in Washington, D.C.

4. *Q.* Do you know the names of the first three Presidents?
   A. Yes: George Washington, John Adams, and Thomas Jefferson.

5. *Q.* Who wrote the pledge to the flag of the United States (Pledge of Allegiance)?
   A. Francis Bellamy.

6. *Q.* Who elects the President?
   A. The people, through the Electoral College.

7. *Q.* In what state are you now living?
   A. In ——— *(give the name of your state).*

8. *Q.* Who makes the laws in your state?
   A. The State Legislature.

9. *Q.* Did we have a government before the Constitution?
   A. Yes, we had a government under the Articles of Confederation.

10. *Q.* What is the 22nd Amendment?
    A. The president can serve only 2 terms.

11. *Q.* What are the divisions of Congress?
    A. The Senate and the House of Representatives.

12. *Q.* What body advises the President in making policy decisions?
    A. A cabinet made up of 11 members.

13. *Q.* Can the President make treaties with other nations?
    A. Yes, he can make treaties with the consent of the Senate.

14. *Q.* What is the 26th Amendment?
    A. That a person 18 years of age or older can vote.

15. *Q.* What do you pledge when you stand before the national flag?
    A. *I pledge allegiance to the flag of the United States of America, and to the Republic for which it stands; one nation under God, indivisible, with liberty and justice for all.*

16. *Q.* How does an amendment become part of the Constitution?
    A. It is passed by Congress with a two-thirds vote and by a three-fourths vote in the State Legislatures.

17. *Q.* What is your nationality?
    A. *(Give correct answer.)*

18. *Q.* In order, name the successors to the President in case the President resigns or dies.
    A. 1. The Vice President
       2. The Speaker of the House.
       3. The President *pro tempore* of the Senate.

19. *Q.* What does impeachment mean?
    A. It means officially accusing an officer of wrongdoing and forcing that official to resign.

20. *Q.* How long does a Federal judge serve?
    A. For life, unless he or she is charged with unbecoming conduct.

21. *Q.* What is the 20th Amendment?
    A. It changed the date of the President's inauguration to January 20 and the opening date of Congress to January 3.

22. *Q.* (a) What is the Legislative Branch of the United States government?
    A.   The Congress.
    Q. (b) What is the Executive Branch?
    A.   The President and his Cabinet.
    Q. (c) What is the Judicial Branch?
    A.   The courts.

23. *Q.* Can Congress pass a bill in spite of the President's veto?
    A. Yes, by a two-thirds majority of Congress.

24. *Q.* Who appoints the justices of the Supreme Court?
    A. The President, with the consent of the Senate.

25. *Q.* What are the qualifications for Vice President?
    A. The same as for the President.

26. *Q.* What are the principles of the United States Constitution?
    A. Liberty, equality, and justice.

27. *Q.* What are the first 10 Amendments called?
    A. The Bill of Rights.

28. *Q.* What is a democratic government?
    A. Government by the people through their elected representatives.

29. *Q.* What are the qualifications for United States Senator?
    A. A Senator must be an American citizen, 30 years old or

more. He or she must have lived in the United States for more than nine (9) years as an American citizen.

30. Q. What are the qualifications for United States Representative (Congressman)?
    A. A Representative must be an American citizen, 25 years old or more, who has lived in the United States for more than seven (7) years as an American citizen.

31. Q. What is meant by a Presidential veto?
    A. It is the President's refusal to sign a bill which has been passed by Congress.

32. Q. Is the American government a federation or centralized?
    A. It is a federation.

33. Q. Who makes the laws for each of the 50 states?
    A. The state legislature of each state.

34. Q. Who is the head of the Supreme Court?
    A. The Chief Justice.

35. Q. What are the major political parties in the United States?
    A. The Democratic party and the Republican party.

36. Q. Has any President been impeached?
    A. Yes. Andrew Johnson was impeached in 1868, but he was not convicted.

37. Q. Who is the head of the Armed Forces?
    A. The President.

38. Q. Can the President declare war?
    A. No.

39. Q. Can any state make a treaty or alliance with a foreign country?
    A. No, only the Federal Government can do so.

40. *Q.* What is the 16th Amendment?
    A. It allows the government to tax incomes.

41. *Q.* What is the 19th Amendment?
    A. It gives women the right to vote.

42. *Q.* How many Senators are there in Congress?
    A. There are 100.

43. *Q.* How many Amendments are there to the United States Constitution?
    A. There are 26 Amendments.

44. *Q.* What are the qualifications for President?
    A. The President must be over 35 years of age and a native-born citizen, who has lived in the United States for more than 14 years.

45. *Q.* Is the United States a dictatorship, a monarchy, or a republic?
    A. The United States is a republic.

46. *Q.* How many Representatives does each state have?
    A. The number depends on the population of each state.

47. *Q.* How many Senators does each state have?
    A. Each state has two (2) Senators.

48. *Q.* Who is the President of the United States at present?
    A. *(Give correct name of person now holding office.)*

49. *Q.* Who is the Vice President of the United States?
    A. *(Give correct name of person now holding office.)*

50. *Q.* Do you know the current population of the United States?
    A. Around 200 million.

51. *Q.* How long is a term in office for the President?
    A. Four years.

52. *Q.* How long is the term for a Senator?
    A. Six years.

53. *Q.* How long is the term for a Representative?
    A. Two years.

54. *Q.* What is an Amendment?
    A. It is a change or an addition to the Constitution.

55. *Q.* Who makes the laws of the United States?
    A. The Congress.

56. *Q.* If the President dies or cannot perform his duties, who takes his place?
    A. The Vice President.

57. *Q.* What are the three United States courts?
    A. 1. The United States Supreme Court.
    2. The United States Circuit Court.
    3. The United States District Court.

58. *Q.* What is the highest court in the United States?
    A. It is the United States Supreme Court.

59. *Q.* How many justices are there in the United States Supreme Court?
    A. There are nine justices.

60. *Q.* What are the three branches of the United States government?
    A. 1. Legislative.
    2. Executive.
    3. Judicial.

61. *Q.* How are the State Representatives selected?
    A. They are elected by registered voters within each state.

62. *Q.* Who is the Governor of your state?
    A. *(Give correct name of person now holding office.)*

63. *Q.* Name one Congressman and one Senator from your state.
    A. *(Give correct names of the people holding these offices.)*

64. *Q.* When was your state admitted to the Union?
    A. *(Give correct date for the state in which you live.)*

65. *Q.* Where is the United States Supreme Court located?
    A. In Washington, D.C.

66. *Q.* What is the Cabinet?
    A. It is a group of people selected by the President and approved by the Senate who assist the President in special areas such as agriculture, commerce, foreign affairs, etc.

67. *Q.* Do you know the name of the bird that is the symbol of the United States?
    A. Yes, the bald eagle.

68. *Q.* What were the Articles of Confederation?
    A. They were the first Constitution of the United States.

69. *Q.* Who is Chief Executive of the United States?
    A. The President.

70. *Q.* Who said the following famous words? "Government of the people, by the people, for the people."
    A. Abraham Lincoln, in the Gettysburg Address (1863).

71. *Q.* Why were the Articles of Confederation discarded in favor of the present Constitution?
    A. Because Congress could make laws but could not enforce them, and there was no unity among the states.

72. *Q.* Can the residents of Washington, D.C., vote?
    A. Yes, in Federal elections and for mayor.

73. *Q.* What United States officials are elected by the people?
    A. The President, Vice President, Senators, and Representatives.

74. *Q.* Why do you want to become an American citizen?
    A. 1. *Example:* Because I am married to a person who is an American citizen.
       2. *Example:* Because I like the freedom and democracy of the United States.

General Information

Sample Sentences

Write the following sentences, completing those which have blanks for answer choices.

1. I want to be an American citizen.

2. I have studied the American Constitution.

3. I have a pen in my right hand.

4. Today is a beautiful day.

5. This pen has———*(blue, black)* ink.

6. I went to a citizenship school for two months.

7. There are three colors in our flag: red, white, and blue.

8. There are fifty (50) states in the United States.

9. I came to———*(state)* from———*(country)* on———*(April 5th) (yesterday) (last week)*.

10. I am wearing a———*(blue, red, green)* dress.

11. I am here to take my test today.

12. Yesterday was a———*(cold, warm, hot)* day.

13. I can read, write, and speak simple English.

14. There are many cars on the street.

15. I am working at———.

16. I am wearing———(*yellow, brown, gray*) shoes.

17. It is raining now.

18. I have been married for———years.

19. We do not have any children (yet).

20. We have———children:———sons and———daughters.

21. We have———son (s).

22. My first name is———.

23. I was married———years ago.

24. May I write something else?

25. I will do my best to be a worthy citizen.

26. I enjoy my work.

Immigration and Naturalization Service

District Offices

Alaska
U.S. Post Office & Courthouse
Building, Room 143
Anchorage, Alaska 99501

Arizona
230 North First Avenue
Phoenix, Arizona 85025

California
300 North Los Angeles Street
Los Angeles, California 90012

Appraisers Building
630 Sansome Street
San Francisco, California 94111

Colorado
17027 Federal Office Building
Denver, Colorado 80202

Connecticut
135 High Street
P.O. Box 1724
Hartford, Connecticut 06101

Florida
Room 1402, Federal Building
51 S.W. First Avenue
Miami, Florida 33130

Georgia
881 Peachtree Street, N.E.
Atlanta, Georgia 30309

Hawaii
595 Ala Moana Boulevard
P.O. Box 461
Honolulu, Hawaii 96809

Illinois
Courthouse & Federal Office Building
219 South Dearborn Street
Chicago, Illinois 60604

Louisiana
New Federal Building
701 Loyola Avenue
New Orleans, Louisiana 70113

Maine
319 U.S. Courthouse
P.O. Box 578
Portland, Maine 04112

Maryland
707 North Calvert Street
Baltimore, Maryland 21202

Massachusetts
150 Tremont Street
Boston, Massachusetts 02111

Michigan
Federal Building
333 Mount Elliott Street
Detroit, Michigan 48207

Minnesota
1014 New Post Office Building
180 E. Kellogg Boulevard
St. Paul, Minnesota 55101

Missouri
819 U.S. Courthouse
811 Grand Avenue
Kansas City, Missouri 64106

Montana
Federal Building
P.O. Box 1724
Helena, Montana 59601

Nebraska
New Federal Building
215 North 17th Street
Omaha, Nebraska 68102

New Jersey
1060 Broad Street
Newark, New Jersey 07102

New York
68 Court Street
Buffalo, New York 14202

20 West Broadway
New York, New York 10007

Ohio
600 Standard Building
1370 Ontario Street
Cleveland, Ohio 44113

Oregon
333 U.S. Courthouse
Broadway & Main Streets
Portland, Oregon 97205

Pennsylvania
128 North Broad Street
Philadelphia, Pennsylvania 19102

Texas
343 U.S. Courthouse
P.O. Box 9398
El Paso, Texas 79984

Route 3
Los Fresnos, Texas 78566

U.S. Post Office & Courthouse
P.O. Box 2539
San Antonio, Texas 78206

Vermont
45 Kingman Street
St. Albans, Vermont 05478

Washington, D.C.
1025 Vermont Avenue, N.W.
Washington, D.C. 20536

Washington
815 Airport Way, S.
Seattle, Washington 98134

Puerto Rico
804 Ponce de Leon Avenue
Santurce
San Juan, Puerto Rico 00908

The Declaration of Independence

In Congress, July 4, 1776

The Unanimous Declaration of the Thirteen United States of America

When in the course of human events, it becomes necessary for one people to dissolve the political bands which have connected them with another, and to assume among the powers of the earth, the separate and equal station to which the laws of Nature and of Nature's God entitle them, a decent respect to the opinions of mankind requires that they should declare the causes which impel them to the separation.

We hold these truths to be self-evident, that all men are created equal, that they are endowed by their Creator with certain unalienable rights, that among these are life, liberty and the pursuit of happiness. That to secure these rights, governments are instituted among men, deriving their just powers from the consent of the governed,—That whenever any form of government becomes destructive of these ends, it is the right of the people to alter or to abolish it, and to institute new government, laying its foundation on such principles and organizing its powers in such form, as to them shall seem most likely to effect their safety and happiness. Prudence, indeed, will dictate that governments long established should not be changed for light and transient causes; and accordingly all experience hath shown, that man-kind are more disposed to suffer, while evils are sufferable, than to right themselves by abolishing the forms to which they are accustomed. But when a long train of abuses and usurpations, pursuing invariably the same object evinces a design to reduce them under absolute despotism, it is their right, it is their duty, to throw off such government, and to provide new guards for their future security.—Such has been the patient sufferance of these Colonies; and such is now the necessity which constrains them to alter their former systems of government. The history of the present King of Great Britain is a history of repeated injuries and usurpations, all having in direct object the establishment of an absolute tyranny over these States. To prove this, let facts be submitted to a candid world.

He has refused his assent to laws, the most wholesome and necessary for the public good.

He has forbidden his Governors to pass laws of immediate and pressing importance, unless suspended in their operation till his assent should be obtained; and when so suspended, he has utterly neglected to attend to them.

He has refused to pass other laws for the accommodation of large districts of people, unless those people would relinquish the right of representation in the legislature, a right inestimable to them and formidable to tyrants only.

He has called together legislative bodies at places unusual, uncomfortable, and distant from the depository of their public records, for the sole purpose of fatiguing them into compliance with his measures.

He has dissolved Representative Houses repeatedly, for opposing with manly firmness his invasions on the rights of the people.

He has refused for a long time, after such dissolutions, to cause others to be elected; whereby the legislative powers, incapable of annihilation, have returned to the people at large for their exercise; the State remaining in the mean time exposed to all the dangers of invasion from without, and convulsions within.

He has endeavoured to prevent the population of these States; for that purpose obstructing the laws for naturalization of foreigners; refusing to pass others to encourage their migrations hither, and raising the conditions of new appropriations of lands.

He has obstructed the administration of justice, by refusing his assent to laws for establishing judiciary powers.

He has made judges dependent on his will alone, for the

tenure of their offices, and the amount and payment of their salaries.

He has erected a multitude of new offices, and sent hither swarms of officers to harass our people, and eat out their substance.

He has kept among us, in times of peace, standing armies without the consent of our legislatures.

He has affected to render the military independent of and superior to the civil power.

He has combined with others to subject us to a jurisdiction foreign to our constitution, and unacknowledged by our laws; giving his assent to their acts of pretended legislation:

For quartering large bodies of armed troops among us:

For protecting them, by a mock trial, from punishment for any murders which they should commit on the inhabitants of these States:

For cutting off our trade with all parts of the world:

For imposing taxes on us without our consent:

For depriving us in many cases, of the benefits of trial by jury:

For transporting us beyond seas to be tried for pretended offenses:

For abolishing the free system of English laws in a neighbouring province, establishing therein an arbitrary government, and enlarging its boundaries so as to render it at once an example and fit instrument for introducing the same absolute rule into these colonies:

For taking away our charters, abolishing our most valuable laws, and altering fundamentally the forms of our governments:

For suspending our own legislatures, and declaring themselves invested with power to legislate for us in all cases whatsoever.

He has abdicated government here, by declaring us out of his protection and waging war against us.

He has plundered our seas, ravaged our coasts, burnt our towns, and destroyed the lives of our people.

He is at this time transporting large armies of foreign mercenaries to complete the works of death, desolation and tyranny, already begun with circumstances of cruelty and perfidy scarcely paralleled in the most barbarous ages, and totally unworthy the head of a civilized nation.

He has constrained our fellow citizens taken captive on the high seas to bear arms against their country, to become the executioners of their friends and brethren, or to fall themselves by their hands.

He has excited domestic insurrections amongst us, and has endeavoured to bring on the inhabitants of our frontiers, the merciless Indian savages, whose known rule of warfare is an undistinguished destruction of all ages, sexes and conditions.

In every stage of these oppressions we have petitioned for redress in the most humble terms: Our repeated petitions have been answered only by repeated injury. A prince, whose character is thus marked by every act which may define a tyrant, is unfit to be the ruler of a free people.

Nor have we been wanting in attentions to our British brethren. We have warned them from time to time of attempts by their legislature to extend an unwarrantable jurisdiction over us. We have reminded them of the circumstances of our emigration and settlement here. We have appealed to their native justice and magnanimity, and we have conjured them by the ties of our common kindred to disavow these usurpations, which, would inevitably interrupt our connections and correspondence. They too have been deaf to the voice of justice and of consanguinity. We must, therefore, acquiesce in the necessity which denounces our separation, and hold them, as we hold the rest of mankind, enemies in war, in peace friends.

WE, THEREFORE, the Representatives of the United States of America, in General Congress, Assembled, appealing to the Supreme Judge of the world for the rectitude of our intentions, do, in the name, and by authority of the good people of these Colonies, solemnly publish and declare, That these United Colonies are, and of right ought to be FREE AND INDEPENDENT STATES; that they are absolved from all allegiance to the British Crown, and that all political connection between them and the State of Great Britain, is and ought to be totally dissolved; and that as free and independent States, they have full power to levy war, conclude peace, contract alliances, establish commerce, and to do all other acts and things which independent States may of right do. And for the support of this Declaration, with a firm reliance on the protection of Divine Providence, we mutually pledge to each other our lives, our fortunes and our sacred honor.

John Hancock.

New Hampshire

Josiah Bartlett	Matthew Thornton
Wm. Whipple	

Massachusetts Bay

Saml. Adams	Robt. Treat Paine
John Adams	Elbridge Gerry

Rhode Island

Step. Hopkins	William Ellery

Connecticut

Roger Sherman	Wm. Williams
Saml. Huntington	Oliver Wolcott

New York

Wm. Floyd	Frans. Lewis
Phil. Livingston	Lewis Morris

New Jersey

Richd. Stockton	John Hart
Jno. Witherspoon	Abra. Clark
Fras. Hopkinson	

Pennsylvania

Robt. Morris	Jas. Smith
Benjamin Rush	Geo. Taylor

Benja. Franklin
John Morton
Geo. Clymer

James Wilson
Geo. Ross

Delaware

Caesar Rodney
Geo. Read

Tho. M'Kean

Maryland

Samuel Chase
Wm. Paca
Thos. Stone

Charles Carroll
of Carrollton

Virginia

George Wythe
Richard Henry Lee
Th. Jefferson
Benja. Harrison

Thos. Nelson Jr.
Francis Lightfoot Lee
Carter Braxton

North Carolina

Wm. Hooper
Joseph Hewes

John Penn

South Carolina

Edward Rutledge
Thos. Heyward Junr.

Thomas Lynch Junr.
Arthur Middleton

Georgia

Button Gwinnett
Lyman Hall

Geo. Walton

Constitution of the United States of America

PREAMBLE

WE THE PEOPLE of the United States, in order to form a more perfect Union, establish justice, insure domestic tranquility, provide for the common defense, promote the general welfare, and secure the blessings of liberty to ourselves and our posterity, do ordain and establish this Constitution for the United States of America.

ARTICLE I

SECTION 1. All legislative powers herein granted shall be vested in a Congress of the United States, which shall consist of a Senate and House of Representatives.

SECTION 2. The House of Representatives shall be composed of members chosen every second year by the people of the several States, and the electors in each State shall have the qualifications requisite for electors of the most numerous branch of the State Legislature.

No person shall be a representative who shall not have attained to the age of twenty-five years, and been seven years a citizen of the United States, and who shall not, when elected, be an inhabitant of that State in which he shall be chosen.

Representatives and direct taxes shall be apportioned among the several States which may be included within this Union, according to their respective numbers, which shall be determined by adding to the whole number of free persons, including those bound to service for a term of years, and excluding Indians not taxed, three-fifths of all other persons. The actual enumeration shall be made within three years after the first meeting of the Congress of the United States, and within every subsequent term of ten years, in such manner as they shall by law direct. The number of representatives shall not exceed one for every thirty thousand, but each State shall have at least one representative; and until such enumeration shall be made, the State of New Hampshire shall be entitled to choose three, Massachusetts eight, Rhode Island and Providence Plantations one, Connecticut five, New York six, New Jersey four, Pennsylvania eight, Delaware one, Maryland six, Virginia ten, North Carolina five, South Carolina five, and Georgia three.

When vacancies happen in the representation from any State, the Executive authority thereof shall issue writs of election to fill such vacancies.

The House of Representatives shall choose their Speaker and other officers; and shall have the sole power of impeachment.

SECTION 3. The Senate of the United States shall be composed of two senators from each State, chosen by the legislature thereof, for six years and each senator shall have one vote.

Immediately after they shall be assembled in consequence of the first election, they shall be divided as equally as may be into three classes. The seats of the senators of the first class shall be vacated at the expiration of the second year, of the second class at the expiration of the fourth year, and of the third class at the expiration of the sixth year, so that one-third may be chosen every second year; and if vacancies happen by resignation, or otherwise, during the recess of the legislature of any State, the executive thereof may make temporary appointments until the next meeting of the legislature, which shall then fill such vacancies.

No person shall be a senator who shall not have attained to the age of thirty years, and been nine years a citizen of the United States, and who shall not, when elected, be an inhabitant of that State for which he shall be chosen.

The Vice President of the United States shall be President of the Senate, but shall have no vote, unless they be equally divided.

The Senate shall choose their other officers, and also a President pro tempore, in the absence of the Vice President, or when he shall exercise the office of President of the United States.

The Senate shall have the sole power to try all impeachments. When sitting for that purpose, they shall be on oath or affirmation. When the President of the United States is tried, the Chief Justice shall preside: And no person shall be convicted without the concurrence of two thirds of the members present.

Judgment in cases of impeachment shall not extend further than to removal from office, and disqualification to hold and enjoy any office or honor, trust or profit under the United States: but the party convicted shall nevertheless be liable and subject to indictment, trial, judgment and punishment, according to law.

SECTION 4. The times, places and manner of holding elections for senators and representatives, shall be prescribed in each State by the legislature thereof; but the Congress may at any time by law make or alter such regulations, except as to the places of choosing senators.

The Congress shall assemble at least once in every year, and such meeting shall be on the first Monday in December, unless they shall by law appoint a different day.

SECTION 5. Each house shall be the judge of the elections, returns and qualifications of its own members, and a majority of each shall constitute a quorum to do business; but a smaller number may adjourn from day to day, and may be authorized to compel the attendance of absent members, in such manner, and under such penalties as each house may provide.

Each house may determine the rules of its proceedings, punish its members for disorderly behaviour, and, with the concurrence of two-thirds, expel a member.

Each house shall keep a journal of its proceedings, and from time to time publish the same, excepting such parts as may in their judgment require secrecy; and the yeas and the nays of the members of either house on any question shall, at the desire of one-fifth of those present, be entered on the journal.

Neither house, during the session of Congress, shall, without the consent of the other, adjourn for more than three days, nor to any other place than that in which the two houses shall be sitting.

SECTION 6. The senators and representatives shall receive a

compensation for their services, to be ascertained by law, and paid out of the Treasury of the United States. They shall in all cases, except treason, felony and breach of the peace, be privileged from arrest during their attendance at the session of their respective houses, and in going to and returning from the same; and for any speech or debate in either house, they shall not be questioned in any other place.

No senator or representative shall, during the time for which he was elected, be appointed to any civil office under the authority of the United States, which shall have been created, or the emoluments whereof shall have been increased during such time; and no person holding any office under the United States, shall be a member of either house during his continuance in office.

SECTION 7. All bills for raising revenue shall originate in the House of Representatives; but the Senate may propose or concur with amendments as on other bills.

Every bill which shall have passed the House of Representatives and the Senate, shall, before it become a law, be presented to the President of the United States; if he approves he shall sign it, but if not he shall return it, with his objections to that house in which it shall have originated, who shall enter for the objections at large on their journal, and proceed to reconsider it. If after such reconsideration two thirds of that House shall agree to pass the bill, it shall be sent, together with the objections, to the other House, by which it shall likewise be reconsidered, and if approved by two thirds of that House, it shall become a law. But in all cases the votes of both Houses shall be determined by yeas and nays, and the names of the persons voting for and against the bill shall be entered on the journal of each House respectively. If any bill shall not be returned by the President within ten days (Sundays excepted) after it shall have been presented to him, the same shall be a law, in like manner as if he had signed it, unless the Congress by their adjournment prevent its return, in which case it shall not be a law.

Every order, resolution, or vote to which the concurrence of the Senate and House of Representatives may be necessary (except on a question of adjournment) shall be presented to the

President of the United States; and before the same shall take effect, shall be approved by him, or being disapproved by him, shall be repassed by two thirds of the Senate and House of Representatives, according to the rules and limitations prescribed in the case of a bill.

SECTION 8. The Congress shall have power to lay and collect taxes, duties, imposts and excises, to pay the debts and provide for the common defense and general welfare of the United States; but all duties, imposts and excises shall be uniform throughout the United States;

To borrow money on the credit of the United States;

To regulate commerce with foreign nations, and among the several States, and with the Indian tribes;

To establish a uniform rule of naturalization, and uniform laws on the subject of bankruptcies throughout the United States;

To coin money, regulate the value thereof, and of foreign coin, and fix the standard of weights and measures;

To provide for the punishment of counterfeiting the securities and current coin of the United States;

To establish post offices and post roads;

To promote the progress of science and useful arts, by securing for limited times to authors and inventors the exclusive right to their respective writings and discoveries;

To constitute tribunals inferior to the Supreme Court;

To define and punish piracies and felonies committed on the high seas, and offenses against the law of nations;

To declare war, grant letters of marque and reprisal, and make rules concerning captures on land and water;

To raise and support armies, but no appropriation of money to that use shall be for a longer term than two years;

To provide and maintain a Navy;

To make rules for the government and regulation of the land and naval forces;

To provide for calling forth the militia to execute the laws of the Union, suppress insurrections and repel invasions;

To provide for organizing, arming, and disciplining the militia, and for governing such part of them as may be employed in the service of the United States, reserving to the States respectively, the appointment of the officers, and the authority of training the militia according to the discipline prescribed by Congress;

To exercise exclusive legislation in all cases whatsoever, over such district (not exceeding ten miles square) as may, by cession of particular States, and the acceptance of Congress, become the seat of the Government of the United States, and to exercise like authority over all places purchased by the consent of the legislature of the State in which the same shall be, for the erection of forts, magazines, arsenals, dock-yards, and other needful buildings;—And

To make all laws which shall be necessary and proper for carrying into execution the foregoing powers and all other powers vested by this Constitution in the Government of the United States, or in any department or officer thereof.

SECTION 9. The migration of importation of such persons as any of the States now existing shall think proper to admit, shall not be prohibited by the Congress prior to the year one thousand eight hundred and eight, but a tax or duty may be imposed on such importation, not exceeding ten dollars for each person.

The privilege of the writ of habeas corpus shall not be suspended, unless when in cases of rebellion or invasion the public safety may require it.

No bill of attainder or ex post facto law shall be passed.

No capitation, or other direct, tax shall be laid, unless in proportion to the census or enumeration herein before directed to be taken.

No tax or duty shall be laid on articles exported from any State.

No preference shall be given by any regulation of commerce or revenue to the ports of one State over those of another: nor shall vessels bound to, or from, one State, be obliged to enter, clear, or pay duties in another.

No money shall be drawn from the Treasury, but in consequence of appropriations made by law; and a regular statement and account of the receipts and expenditures of all public money shall be published from time to time.

No title of nobility shall be granted by the United States:

And no person holding any office of profit or trust under them, shall, without the consent of the Congress, accept of any present, emolument, office, or title, of any kind whatever, from any King, Prince, or foreign State.

SECTION 10. No State shall enter into any treaty, alliance, or confederation, grant letters of marque and reprisal; coin money; emit bills of credit; make any thing but gold and silver coin a tender in payment of debts; pass any bill of attainder, ex post facto law, or law impairing the obligation of contracts, or grant any title of nobility.

No State shall, without the consent of the Congress, lay any imposts or duties on imports or exports, except what may be absolutely necessary for executing its inspection laws: and the net produce of all duties and imposts, laid by any State on imports or exports, shall be for the use of the Treasury of the United States; and all such laws shall be subject to the revision and control of the Congress.

No State shall, without the consent of Congress, lay any duty of tonnage, keep troops, or ships of war in time of peace, enter into any agreement or compact with another State, or with a foreign power, or engage in war, unless actually invaded, or in such imminent danger as will not admit of delay.

ARTICLE II

SECTION 1. The executive power shall be vested in a President of the United States of America. He shall hold his office during the term of four years, and, together with the Vice President, chosen for the same term, be elected, as follows:

Each State, shall appoint, in such manner as the legislature thereof may direct, a number of electors, equal to the whole number of senators and representatives to which the State may be entitled in the Congress; but no senator or representative, or person holding an office of trust or profit under the United States, shall be appointed an elector.

The electors shall meet in their respective States, and vote by ballot for two persons, of whom one at least shall not be an inhabitant of the same State with themselves. And they shall make a list of all the persons voted for, and of the number of votes for each; which list they shall sign and certify, and transmit sealed to the seat of the Government of the United States, directed to the President of the Senate. The President of the Senate shall, in the presence of the Senate and House of Representatives, open all the certificates, and the votes shall then be counted. The person having the greatest number of votes shall be the President, if such number be a majority of the whole number of electors appointed; and if there be more than one who have such majority, and have an equal number of votes, then the House of Representatives shall immediately choose by ballot one of them for President; and if no person have a majority, then from the five highest on the list the said House shall in like manner choose the President. But in choosing the President, the votes shall be taken by States, the representation from each State having one vote; a quorum for this purpose shall consist of a member or members from two thirds of the States, and a majority of all the States shall be necessary to a choice. In every case, after the choice of the President, the person having the greatest number of votes of the electors shall be the Vice President. But if there should remain two or more who have equal votes, the Senate shall choose from them by ballot the Vice President.

The Congress may determine the time of choosing the electors, and the day on which they shall give their votes; which day shall be the same throughout the United States.

No person except a natural born citizen, or a citizen of the United States, at the time of the adoption of this Constitution, shall be eligible to the office of President; neither shall any person be eligible to that office who shall not have attained to the age of thirty-five years, and been fourteen years a resident within the United States.

In case of the removal of the President from office, or of his death, resignation, or inability to discharge the powers and duties of the said office, the same shall devolve on the Vice President, and the Congress may by law provide for the case of removal, death, resignation, or inability, both of the President and Vice President, declaring what officer shall then act as President, and such officer shall act accordingly, until the disability be removed, or a President shall be elected.

The President shall, at stated times, receive for his services, a compensation, which shall neither be increased nor diminished during the period for which he shall have been elected, and he shall not receive within that period any other emolument from the United States, or any of them.

Before he enter on the execution of his office, he shall take the following oath or affirmation:—"I do solemnly swear (or affirm) that I will faithfully execute the office of President of the United States, and will to the best of my ability, preserve, protect and defend the Constitution of the United States."

SECTION 2. The President shall be Commander in Chief of the Army and Navy of the United States, and of the militia of the several States, when called into the actual service of the United States; he may require the opinion, in writing, of the principal officer in each of the Executive Departments, upon any subject relating to the duties of their respective offices, and he shall have power to grant reprieves and pardons for offenses against the United States, except in cases of impeachment.

He shall have power, by and with the advice and consent of the Senate, to make treaties, provided two-thirds of the Senators present concur; and he shall nominate, and by and with the advice and consent of the Senate, shall appoint ambassadors, other public ministers and consuls, Judges of the Supreme Court, and all other officers of the United States, whose appointments are not herein otherwise provided for, and which shall be established by law: but the Congress may by law vest the appointment of such inferior officers, as they think proper, in the President alone, in the courts of law, or in the heads of departments.

The President shall have power to fill up all vacancies that may happen during the recess of the Senate, by granting commissions which shall expire at the end of their next session.

SECTION 3. He shall from time to time give to the Congress information of the state of the Union, and recommend to their consideration such measures as he shall judge necessary and expedient; he may, on extraordinary occasions, convene both houses, or either of them, and in case of disagreement between them, with respect to the time of adjournment, he may adjourn them to such time as he shall think proper; he shall receive ambassadors and other public ministers; he shall take care that the laws be faithfully executed, and shall commission all the officers of the United States.

SECTION 4. The President, Vice President and all civil officers of the United States, shall be removed from office on impeachment for, and conviction of, treason, bribery, or other high crimes and misdemeanors.

ARTICLE III

SECTION 1. The judicial power of the United States, shall be vested in one Supreme Court, and in such inferior courts as the Congress may from time to time ordain and establish. The judges, both of the supreme and inferior courts, shall hold their offices during good behaviour, and shall, at stated times, receive for their services, a compensation, which shall not be diminished during their continuance in office.

SECTION 2. The judicial power shall extend to all cases, in law and equity, arising under this Constitution, the laws of the United States, and treaties made, or which shall be made, under their authority;—to all cases affecting ambassadors, other public ministers and consuls;—to all cases of admiralty and maritime jurisdiction;—to controversies to which the United States shall be a party;—to controversies between two or more States;—between a State and citizens of another State;—between citizens of different States,—between citizens of the same State claiming lands under grants of different States, and between a State, or the citizens thereof, and foreign States, citizens or subjects.

In all cases affecting ambassadors, other public ministers and consuls, and those in which a State shall be a party, the Supreme Court shall have original jurisdiction. In all the other cases before mentioned, the Supreme Court shall have appellate jurisdiction, both as to law and fact, with such exceptions, and under such regulations as the Congress shall make.

The trial of all crimes, except in cases of impeachment, shall be by jury; and such trial shall be held in the State where the said crimes shall have been committed; but when not committed within any State, the trial shall be at such place or places as the Congress may by law have directed.

SECTION 3. Treason against the United States, shall consist only in levying war against them, or in adhering to their enemies, giving them aid and comfort. No person shall be convicted of treason unless on the testimony of two witnesses to the same overt act, or on confession in open court.

The Congress shall have power to declare the punishment of treason, but no attainder of treason shall work corruption of blood, or forfeiture except during the life of the person attained.

ARTICLE IV

SECTION 1. Full faith and credit shall be given in each State to the public acts, records, and judicial proceedings of every other State. And the Congress may by general laws prescribe the manner in which such acts, records and proceedings shall be proved, and the effect thereof.

SECTION 2. The citizens of each State shall be entitled to all privileges and immunities of citizens in the several States.

A person charged in any State with treason, felony, or other crime, who shall flee from justice, and be found in another State, shall on demand of the executive authority of the State from which he fled, be delivered up, to be removed to the State having jurisdiction of the crime.

No person held to service or labour in one State, under the laws thereof; escaping into another, shall, in consequence of any law or regulation therein, be discharged from such service or labour, but shall be delivered up on claim of the party to whom such service or labour may be due.

SECTION 3. New States may be admitted by the Congress into this Union; but no new State shall be formed or erected within the jurisdiction of any other State; nor any State be formed by the junction of two or more States, or parts of States, without the consent of the legislatures of the States concerned as well as of the Congress.

The Congress shall have power to dispose of and make all needful rules and regulations respecting the Territory or other property belonging to the United States; and nothing in this Constitution shall be so construed as to prejudice any claims of the United States, or of any particular State.

Section 4. The United States shall guarantee to every State in this Union a republican form of Government, and shall protect each of them against invasion; and on application of the legislature, or of the executive (when the legislature cannot be convened) against domestic violence.

ARTICLE V

The Congress, whenever two third of both Houses shall deem it necessary, shall propose amendments to this Constitution, or on the application of the legislatures of two thirds of the several States, shall call a convention for proposing amendments, which, in either case, shall be valid to all intents and purposes, as part of this Constitution, when ratified by the legislatures of three fourths of the several States, or by conventions in three fourths thereof, as the one or the other mode of ratification may be proposed by the Congress; provided that no amendment which may be made prior to the year one thousand eight hundred and eight shall in any manner affect the first and fourth clauses in the Ninth Section of the First Article; and that no State, without its consent, shall be deprived of its equal suffrage in the Senate.

ARTICLE VI

All debts contracted and engagements entered into, before the adoption of this Constitution, shall be as valid against the United States under this Constitution, as under the Confederation.

This Constitution, and the laws of the United States which shall be made in pursuance thereof; and all treaties made, or which shall be made, under the authority of the United States, shall be the supreme law of the land; and the judges in every State shall be bound thereby, any thing in the Constitution or laws of any State to the contrary notwithstanding.

The senators and representatives before mentioned, and the members of the several State legislatures, and all executive and judicial officers, both of the United States and of the several States, shall be bound by oath or affirmation, to support this Constitution; but no religious test shall ever be required as a qualification to any office or public trust under the United States.

ARTICLE VII

The ratification of the conventions of nine States shall be sufficient for the establishment of this Constitution between the States so ratifying the same.

Done in convention by the unanimous consent of the States present the seventeenth day of September in the year of our Lord one thousand seven hundred and eighty seven and of the Independence of the United States of America the twelfth. In witness whereof we have hereunto subscribed our names,

Go. Washington—*Presid't.*
and deputy from Virginia

Attest William Jackson—*Secretary*

New Hampshire

John Langdon	Nicholas Gilman

Massachusetts

Nathaniel Gorham	Rufus King

Connecticut

Wm. Saml. Johnson	Roger Sherman

New York

Alexander Hamilton

New Jersey

Wil: Livingston	Wm. Paterson
David Brearley	Jona: Dayton

Pennsylvania

B. Franklin	Thos. FitzSimons
Thomas Mifflin	Jared Ingersoll
Robt. Morris	James Wilson
Geo. Clymer	Gouv. Morris

Delaware

Geo: Read	Richard Bassett
Gunning Bedford Jun	Jaco: Broom
John Dickinson	

Maryland

James McHenry	Danl. Carroll
Dan. of St. Thos. Jenifer	

Virginia

John Blair—   James Madison Jr.

North Carolina

Wm. Blount   Hu. Williamson
Richd. Dobbs Spaight

South Carolina

J. Rutledge   Charles Pinckney
Charles Cotesworth Pinckney   Pierce Butler

Georgia

William Few   Abr. Baldwin

Amendments

ARTICLE I

Congress shall make no law respecting an establishment of religion, or prohibiting the free exercise thereof; or abridging the freedom of speech, or of the press; or the right of the people peaceably to assemble, and to petition the Government for a redress of grievances.

ARTICLE II

A well regulated militia, being necessary to the security of a free State, the right of the people to keep and bear arms, shall not be infringed.

ARTICLE III

No soldier shall, in time of peace be quartered in any house, without the consent of the owner, nor in time of war, but in a manner to be prescribed by law.

ARTICLE IV

The right of the people to be secure in their persons, houses, papers, and effects, against unreasonable searches and seizures, shall not be violated, and no warrants shall issue, but upon probable cause, supported by oath or affirmation, and particularly describing the place to be searched, and the persons or things to be seized.

ARTICLE V

No person shall be held to answer for a capital, or otherwise infamous crime, unless on a presentment or indictment of a Grand Jury, except in cases arising in the land or naval forces, or in the militia, when in actual service in time of war or public danger; nor shall any person be subject for the same offense to be twice put in jeopardy of life or limb; nor shall be compelled in any criminal case to be a witness against himself, nor be deprived of life, liberty, or property, without due process of law; nor shall private property be taken for public use, without just compensation.

ARTICLE VI

In all criminal prosecutions, the accused shall enjoy the right to a speedy and public trial, by an impartial jury of the State and district wherein the crime shall have been committed, which district shall have been previously ascertained by law, and to be informed of the nature and cause of the accusation; to be confronted with the witnesses against him; to have compulsory process for obtaining witnesses in his favor, and to have the assistance of counsel for his defense.

ARTICLE VII

In suits at common law, where the value in controversy shall exceed twenty dollars, the right of trial by jury shall be preserved, and no fact tried by a jury, shall be otherwise reexamined in any court of the United States, than according to the rules of the common law.

ARTICLE VIII

Excessive bail shall not be required, nor excessive fines imposed, nor cruel and unusual punishments inflicted.

ARTICLE IX

The enumeration in the Constitution, of certain rights, shall not be construed to deny or disparage others retained by the people.

ARTICLE X

The powers not delegated to the United States by the Constitution, nor prohibited by it to the States, are reserved to the States respectively, or to the people.

ARTICLE XI

The judicial power of the United States shall not be construed to extend to any suit in law or equity, commenced or prosecuted against one of the United States by citizens of another State, or by citizens or subjects of any foreign State.

ARTICLE XII

The electors shall meet in their respective States, and vote by ballot for President and Vice President, one of whom, at least, shall not be an inhabitant of the same State with themselves; they shall name in their ballots the person voted for as President, and in distinct ballots the person voted for as Vice President, and they shall make distinct lists of all persons voted for as President, and of all persons voted for as Vice President, and of the number of votes for each, which lists they shall sign and certify, and transmit sealed to the seat of the government of the United States, directed to the President of the Senate;—The President of the Senate shall, in the presence of the Senate and House of Representatives, open all the certificates and the votes shall then be counted;—The person having the greatest number of votes for President, shall be the President, if such number be a majority of the whole number of electors appointed; and if no person have such majority, then from the persons having the highest numbers not exceeding three on the list of those voted for as President, the House of Representatives shall choose immediately, by ballot, the President. But in choosing the President, the votes shall be taken by States, the representation from each State having one vote; a quorum for this purpose shall consist of a member or members from two-thirds of the States, and a majority of all the States shall be necessary to a choice. And if the House of Representatives shall not choose a President whenever the right of choice shall devolve upon them, before the fourth day of March next following, then the Vice President shall act as President, as in the case of the death or other constitutional disability of the President.—The person having the greatest number of votes as Vice President, shall be the Vice President, if such number be a majority of the whole number of electors appointed, and if no person have a majority, then from the two highest numbers on the list, the Senate shall choose the Vice President; a quorum for the purpose shall consist of two-thirds of the whole number of Senators, and a majority of the whole number shall be necessary to a choice. But no person constitutionally ineligible to the office of President shall be eligible to that of Vice President of the United States.

ARTICLE XIII

SECTION 1. Neither slavery nor involuntary servitude, except as a punishment for crime whereof the party shall have been duly convicted, shall exist within the United States, or any place subject to their jurisdiction.

SECTION 2. Congress shall have power to enforce this article by appropriate legislation.

ARTICLE XIV

SECTION 1. All persons born or naturalized in the United States, and subject to the jurisdiction thereof, are citizens of the United States and of the State wherein they reside. No State shall make or enforce any law which shall abridge the privileges or immunities of citizens of the United States; nor shall any State deprive any person of life, liberty, or property, without due process of law; nor deny to any person within its jurisdiction the equal protection of the laws.

SECTION 2. Representatives shall be apportioned among the

several States according to their respective numbers, counting the whole number of persons in each State, excluding Indians not taxed. But when the right to vote at any election for the choice of electors for President and Vice President of the United States, Representatives in Congress, the executive and judicial officers of a State, or the members of the legislature thereof, is denied to any of the male inhabitants of such State, being twenty-one years of age, and citizens of the United States, or in any way abridged, except for participation in rebellion, or other crime, the basis of representation therein shall be reduced in the proportion which the number of such male citizens shall bear to the whole number of male citizens twenty-one years of age in such State.

SECTION 3. No person shall be a Senator or Representative in Congress, or elector of President and Vice President, or hold any office, civil or military, under the United States, or under any State, who, having previously taken an oath, as a member of Congress, or as an officer of the United States, or as a member of any State legislature, or as an executive or judicial officer of any State, to support the Constitution of the United States, shall have engaged in insurrection or rebellion against the same, or given aid or comfort to the enemies thereof. But Congress may by a vote of two-thirds of each house, remove such disability.

SECTION 4. The validity of the public debt of the United States, authorized by law, including debts incurred for payment of pensions and bounties for services in suppressing insurrection or rebellion, shall not be questioned. But neither the United States nor any State shall assume or pay any debt or obligation incurred in aid of insurrection or rebellion against the United States, or any claim for the loss or emancipation of any slave; but all such debts, obligations and claims shall be held illegal and void.

SECTION 5. The Congress shall have power to enforce, by appropriate legislation, the provisions of this article.

ARTICLE XV

SECTION 1. The right of citizens of the United States to vote shall not be denied or abridged by the United States or by any

State on account of race, color, or previous condition of servitude.

SECTION 2. The Congress shall have power to enforce this article by appropriate legislation.

ARTICLE XVI

The Congress shall have power to lay and collect taxes on incomes, from whatever source derived, without apportionment among the several States, and without regard to any census or enumeration.

ARTICLE XVII

SECTION 1. The Senate of the United States shall be composed of two senators from each State, elected by the people thereof, for six years; and each senator shall have one vote. The electors in each State shall have the qualifications requisite for electors of the most numerous branch of the State legislatures.

SECTION 2. When vacancies happen in the representation of any State in the senate, the executive authority of such State shall issue writs of election to fill such vacancies: *Provided,* That the legislature of any State may empower the executive thereof to make temporary appointments until the people fill the vacancies by election as the legislature may direct.

SECTION 3. This amendment shall not be so construed as to affect the election or term of any senator chosen before it becomes valid as part of the Constitution.

ARTICLE XVIII

SECTION 1. After one year from the ratification of this article the manufacture, sale, or transportation of intoxicating liquors within, the importation thereof into, or the exportation thereof from the United States and all territory subject to the jurisdiction thereof for beverage purposes is hereby prohibited.

SECTION 2. The Congress and the several States shall have concurrent power to enforce this article by appropriate legislation.

SECTION 3. This article shall be inoperative unless it shall have been ratified as an amendment to the Constitution by the legislatures of the several States, as provided in the Constitution, within seven years from the date of the submission hereof to the States by the Congress.

ARTICLE XIX

SECTION 1. The right of citizens of the United States to vote shall not be denied or abridged by the United States or by any State on account of sex.

ARTICLE XX

SECTION 1. The terms of the President and Vice President shall end at noon on the 20th day of January, and the terms of Senators and Representatives at noon on the 3d day of January, of the years in which such terms would have ended if this article had not been ratified; and the terms of their successors shall then begin.

SECTION 2. The Congress shall assemble at least once in every year, and such meeting shall begin at noon on the 3d day of January, unless they shall by law appoint a different day.

SECTION 3. If, at the time fixed for the beginning of the term of the President, the President elect shall have died, the Vice President elect shall become President. If a President shall not have been chosen before the time fixed for the beginning of his term, or if the President elect shall have failed to qualify, then the Vice President elect shall act as President until a President shall have qualified; and the Congress may by law provide for the case wherein neither a President elect nor a Vice President elect shall have qualified, declaring who shall then act as President, or the manner in which one who is to act shall be selected, and such person shall act accordingly until a President or Vice President shall have qualified.

SECTION 4. The Congress may by law provide for the case of the death of any of the persons from whom the House of Representatives may choose a President whenever the right of choice shall have devolved upon them, and for the case of the death of any of the persons from whom the Senate may choose a Vice President whenever the right of choice shall have devolved upon them.

SECTION 5. Sections 1 and 2 shall take effect on the 15th day of October following the ratification of this article.

SECTION 6. This article shall be inoperative unless it shall have been ratified as an amendment to the Constitution by the legislatures of three-fourths of the several States within seven years from the date of its submission.

ARTICLE XXI

SECTION 1. The eighteenth article of amendment to the Constitution of the United States is hereby repealed.

SECTION 2. The transportation or importation into any State, Territory, or possession of the United States for delivery or use therein of intoxicating liquors, in violation of the laws thereof, is hereby prohibited.

SECTION 3. This article shall be inoperative unless it shall have been ratified as an amendment to the Constitution by conventions in the several States, as provided in the Constitution, within seven years from the date of the submission hereof to the States by the Congress.

ARTICLE XXII

SECTION 1. No person shall be elected to the office of the President more than twice, and no person who has held the office of President, or acted as President, for more than 2 years of a term to which some other person was elected President shall be elected to the office of the President more than once. But this Article shall not apply to any person holding the office of President when this Article was proposed by the Congress, and shall not prevent any person who may be holding the office of President, or acting as President, during the term within which this Article becomes operative from holding the office of President or acting as President during the remainder of such term.

SECTION 2. This Article shall be inoperative unless it shall have been ratified as an amendment to the Constitution by the legislatures of three-fourths of the several States within 7 years from the date of its submission to the States by the Congress.

ARTICLE XXIII

SECTION 1. The District constituting the seat of Government of the United States shall appoint in such manner as the Congress may direct:

A number of electors of President and Vice President equal to the whole number of Senators and Representatives in Congress to which the District would be entitled if it were a State, but in no event more than the least populous State; they shall be in addition to those appointed by the States, but they shall be considered, for the purposes of the election of President and Vice President, to be electors appointed by a State; and they shall meet in the District and perform such duties as provided by the twelfth article of amendment.

SECTION 2. The Congress shall have power to enforce this article by appropriate legislation.

ARTICLE XXIV

SECTION 1. The right of citizens of the United States to vote in any primary or other election for President or Vice President, for electors for President or Vice President, or for Senator or Representative in Congress, shall not be denied or abridged by the United States or any State by reason of failure to pay any poll tax or other tax.

SECTION 2. The Congress shall have power to enforce this article by appropriate legislation.

ARTICLE XXV

SECTION 1. In case of the removal of the President from office or of his death or resignation, the Vice President shall become President.

SECTION 2. Whenever there is a vacancy in the office of the

Vice President, the President shall nominate a Vice President who shall take office upon confirmation by a majority vote of both Houses of Congress.

SECTION 3. Whenever the President transmits to the President pro tempore of the Senate and the Speaker of the House of Representatives his written declaration that he is unable to discharge the powers and duties of his office, and until he transmits to them a written declaration to the contrary, such powers and duties shall be discharged by the Vice President as Acting President.

SECTION 4. Whenever the Vice President and a majority of either the principal officers of the executive departments or of such other body as Congress may by law provide, transmit to the President pro tempore of the Senate and the Speaker of the House of Representatives their written declaration that the President is unable to discharge the powers and duties of his office, the Vice President shall immediately assume the powers and duties of the office as Acting President.

Thereafter, when the President transmits to the President pro tempore of the Senate and the Speaker of the House of Representatives his written declaration that no inability exists, he shall resume the powers and duties of his office unless the Vice President and a majority of either the principal officers of the executive department or of such other body as Congress may by law provide, transmit within four days to the President pro tempore of the Senate and the Speaker of the House of Representatives their written declaration that the President is unable to discharge the powers and duties of his office. Thereupon Congress shall decide the issue, assembling within forty-eight hours for that purpose if not in session. If the Congress, within twenty-one days after receipt of the latter written declaration, or if Congress is not in session, within twenty-one days after Congress is required to assemble, determines by two-thirds vote of both Houses that the President is unable to discharge the powers and duties of his office, the Vice President shall continue to discharge the same as Acting President; otherwise, the President shall resume the powers and duties of his office.

ARTICLE XXVI

SECTION 1. The right of citizens of the United States, who are eighteen years of age or older, to vote shall not be denied or abridged by the United States or by any state on account of age.

SECTION 2. The Congress shall have power to enforce this article by appropriate legislation.

Samples of Forms You Will Be Asked to Fill Out

APPLICANT

	LEAVE BLANK

TYPE OR PRINT ALL INFORMATION IN BLACK
LAST NAME **NAM**   FIRST NAME   MIDDLE NAME

FBI   LEAVE BLANK

NATURE OF PERSON FINGERPRINTED

SIDENCE OF PERSON FINGERPRINTED

ALIASES **AKA**

O
R
I

NYINSNYOO
USINS
NEW YORK, NY

DATE OF BIRTH **DOB**
Month   Day   Year

CITIZENSHIP **CTZ**	SEX	RACE	HGT.	WGT.	EYES	HAIR	PLACE OF BIRTH **POB**

ATE   SIGNATURE OF OFFICIAL TAKING FINGERPRINTS

YOUR NO. **OCA**

LEAVE BLANK

PLOYER AND ADDRESS

FBI NO. **FBI**

CLASS _____

ARMED FORCES NO. **MNU**

ASON FINGERPRINTED

SOCIAL SECURITY NO. **SOC**

REF. _____

MISCELLANEOUS NO. **MNU**

R. THUMB	2. R. INDEX	3. R. MIDDLE	4. R. RING	5. R. LITTLE

L. THUMB	7. L. INDEX	8. L. MIDDLE	9. L. RING	10. L. LITTLE

LEFT FOUR FINGERS TAKEN SIMULTANEOUSLY	L. THUMB	R. THUMB	RIGHT FOUR FINGERS TAKEN SIMULTANEOUSLY

FEDERAL BUREAU OF INVESTIGATION
UNITED STATES DEPARTMENT OF JUSTICE
WASHINGTON, D.C. 20537

APPLICANT

1. LOOP

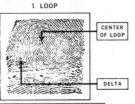

CENTER OF LOOP

DELTA

THE LINES BETWEEN CENTER OF LOOP AND DELTA MUST SHOW

2. WHORL

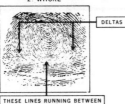

DELTAS

THESE LINES RUNNING BETWEEN DELTAS MUST BE CLEAR

3. ARCH

ARCHES HAVE NO DELTAS

TO OBTAIN CLASSIFIABLE FINGERPRINTS

1. USE BLACK PRINTER'S INK.
2. DISTRIBUTE INK EVENLY ON INKING SLAB.
3. WASH AND DRY FINGERS THOROUGHLY.
4. ROLL FINGERS FROM NAIL TO NAIL, AND AVOID ALLOWING FINGERS TO SLIP.
5. BE SURE IMPRESSIONS ARE RECORDED IN CORRECT ORDER.
6. IF AN AMPUTATION OR DEFORMITY MAKES IT IMPOSSIBLE TO PRINT A FINGER, MAKE A NOTATION TO THAT EFFECT IN THE INDIVIDUAL FINGER BLOCK.
7. IF SOME PHYSICAL CONDITION MAKES IT IMPOSSIBLE TO OBTAIN PERFECT IMPRESSIONS, SUBMIT THE BEST THAT CAN BE OBTAINED WITH A MEMO STAPLED TO THE CARD EXPLAINING THE CIRCUMSTANCES.
8. EXAMINE THE COMPLETED PRINTS TO SEE IF THEY CAN BE CLASSIFIED, BEARING IN MIND THAT MOST FINGERPRINTS FALL INTO THE PATTERNS SHOWN ON THIS CARD (OTHER PATTERNS OCCUR INFREQUENTLY AND ARE NOT SHOWN HERE).

THIS CARD FOR USE BY: LEAVE THIS SPACE BLANK

1. LAW ENFORCEMENT AGENCIES IN FINGERPRINTING APPLICANTS FOR LAW ENFORCEMENT POSITIONS.*

2. OFFICIALS OF STATE AND LOCAL GOVERNMENTS FOR PURPOSES OF EMPLOYMENT, LICENSING, AND PERMITS, AS AUTHORIZED BY STATE STATUTES AND APPROVED BY THE ATTORNEY GENERAL OF THE UNITED STATES. LOCAL AND COUNTY ORDINANCES, UNLESS SPECIFICALLY BASED ON APPLICABLE STATE STATUTES DO NOT SATISFY THIS REQUIREMENT.*

3. U.S. GOVERNMENT AGENCIES AND OTHER ENTITIES REQUIRED BY FEDERAL LAW **

4. OFFICIALS OF FEDERALLY CHARTERED OR INSURED BANKING INSTITUTIONS TO PROMOTE OR MAINTAIN THE SECURITY OF THOSE INSTITUTIONS.

INSTRUCTIONS:

*1. PRINTS MUST FIRST BE CHECKED THROUGH THE APPROPRIATE STATE IDENTIFICATION BUREAU, AND ONLY THOSE FINGERPRINTS FOR WHICH NO DISQUALIFYING RECORD HAS BEEN FOUND LOCALLY SHOULD BE SUBMITTED FOR FBI SEARCH.

2. PRIVACY ACT OF 1974 (P.L. 93-579) REQUIRES THAT FEDERAL, STATE, OR LOCAL AGENCIES INFORM INDIVIDUALS WHOSE SOCIAL SECURITY NUMBER IS REQUESTED WHETHER SUCH DISCLOSURE IS MANDATORY OR VOLUNTARY, BASIS OF AUTHORITY FOR SUCH SOLICITATION, AND USES WHICH WILL BE MADE OF IT.

**3. IDENTITY OF PRIVATE CONTRACTORS SHOULD BE SHOWN IN SPACE "EMPLOYER AND ADDRESS". THE CONTRIBUTOR IS THE NAME OF THE AGENCY SUBMITTING THE FINGERPRINT CARD TO THE FBI.

4. FBI NUMBER, IF KNOWN, SHOULD ALWAYS BE FURNISHED IN THE APPROPRIATE SPACE.

MISCELLANEOUS NO. – RECORD: OTHER ARMED FORCES NO., PASSPORT NO. (PP), ALIEN REGISTRATION NO. (AR), PORT SECURITY CARD NO. (PS), SELECTIVE SERVICE NO. (SS), VETERANS' ADMINISTRATION CLAIM NO. (VA.).

FD 258 (REV. 7-15-77)   ☆ U.S. GOVERNMENT PRINTING OFFICE : 1980 - 317-188

INSTRUCTIONS: USE TYPEWRITER. BE SURE ALL COPIES ARE LEGIBLE. Failure to answer fully all questions delays action.

Do Not Remove Carbons. If typewriter is not available, print heavily in block letters with ball-point pen.

☆ U. S. GOVERNMENT PRINTING OFFICE: 1978—275—704

G-325 (REV. 8-1-74)Y

GRAPHIC
ORMATION

UNITED STATES DEPARTMENT OF JUSTICE

Immigration and Naturalization Service

Form Approved
OMB No. 43-R436

(name)	(First name)	(Middle name)	☐ MALE ☐ FEMALE	BIRTHDATE (Mo.-Day-Yr.)	NATIONALITY	ALIEN REGISTRATION NO. (If any)
OTHER NAMES USED (Including names by previous marriages)			CITY AND COUNTRY OF BIRTH			SOCIAL SECURITY NO. (If any)

	FAMILY NAME	FIRST NAME	DATE, CITY AND COUNTRY OF BIRTH (If known)	CITY AND COUNTRY OF RESIDENCE
THER				
THER (Maiden name)				

BBAND (If none, so state) OR WIFE	FAMILY NAME (For wife, give maiden name)	FIRST NAME	BIRTHDATE	CITY & COUNTRY OF BIRTH	DATE OF MARRIAGE	PLACE OF MARRIAGE

MER HUSBANDS OR WIVES (If none, so state)

MILY NAME (For wife, give maiden name)	FIRST NAME	BIRTHDATE	DATE AND PLACE OF MARRIAGE	DATE AND PLACE OF TERMINATION OF MARRIAGE

PLICANT'S RESIDENCE LAST FIVE YEARS. LIST PRESENT ADDRESS FIRST.

STREET AND NUMBER	CITY	PROVINCE OR STATE	COUNTRY	FROM MONTH	FROM YEAR	TO MONTH	TO YEAR
						PRESENT TIME	

PLICANT'S LAST ADDRESS OUTSIDE THE UNITED STATES OF MORE THAN ONE YEAR.

STREET AND NUMBER	CITY	PROVINCE OR STATE	COUNTRY	FROM MONTH	FROM YEAR	TO MONTH	TO YEAR

PLICANT'S EMPLOYMENT LAST FIVE YEARS. (IF NONE, SO STATE.) LIST PRESENT EMPLOYMENT FIRST.

LL NAME AND ADDRESS OF EMPLOYER	OCCUPATION (Specify)	FROM MONTH	FROM YEAR	TO MONTH	TO YEAR
				PRESENT TIME	

Show below last occupation abroad if not shown above. (Include all information requested above.)

IS FORM IS SUBMITTED IN CONNECTION WITH APPLICATION FOR: ☐ NATURALIZATION ☐ OTHER (SPECIFY) ☐ ADJUSTMENT OF STATUS	SIGNATURE OF APPLICANT OR PETITIONER	DATE

Are all copies legible? ☐ Yes	IF YOUR NATIVE ALPHABET IS IN OTHER THAN ROMAN LETTERS, WRITE YOUR NAME IN YOUR NATIVE ALPHABET IN THIS SPACE:

PENALTIES: SEVERE PENALTIES ARE PROVIDED BY LAW FOR KNOWINGLY AND WILLFULLY FALSIFYING OR CONCEALING A MATERIAL FACT.

APPLICANT:

BE SURE TO PUT YOUR NAME AND ALIEN REGISTRATION NUMBER IN THE BOX OUTLINED BY HEAVY BORDER BELOW.

COMPLETE THIS BOX (Family name)	(Given name)	(Middle name)	(Alien registration number)

(OTHER AGENCY USE)

INS USE (Office of Origin)
OFFICE CODE:
TYPE OF CASE:
DATE:

FORM G-325

[1] Ident.

APPLICATION TO FILE PETITION FOR NATURALIZATION

INSTRUCTIONS TO THE APPLICANT

(Tear off this instruction sheet before filling out this form)

You must be at least 18 years old to file a petition for naturalization. Using ink or a typewriter, answer every question in the application form, whether you are male or female. If you need more space for an answer, write "Continued" in your answer, then finish your answer on a sheet of paper this size, giving the number of the question.

YOU WILL BE EXAMINED UNDER OATH ON THE ANSWERS IN THIS APPLICATION WHEN YOU APPEAR FOR YOUR NATURALIZATION EXAMINATION.

If you wish to be called for examination at the same time as a relative who is applying for naturalization is called, attach a separate sheet so stating, and show the name and the Alien Registration Number of that relative.

1. **YOU MUST SEND WITH THIS APPLICATION THE FOLLOWING ITEMS (1), (2), (3) AND (4):**

(1) **Photographs of your Face:**
   a. Three identical unglazed copies, size 2 x 2 inches only.
   b. Taken within the last 30 days.
   c. Distance from top of head to point of chin to be 1¼ inches.
   d. On thin paper, with light background, showing front view without hat.
   e. In natural color or black and white, and not machine-made.
   f. Unsigned (but write Alien Registration Number lightly in pencil in center of reverse side).

(2) **Fingerprint Chart.**—Complete the personal data items such as name, aliases, weight, date of birth, etc. Write in your Alien Registration Number in the space marked "Miscellaneous No. MNO" or "Your No. OCA" and take the chart with these instructions to any police station, sheriff's office, or office of the Immigration and Naturalization Service for fingerprinting. You must then sign the chart in the presence of the officer taking the fingerprints and have him/her sign his/her name and title and fill in the date in the spaces provided. DO NOT BEND, FOLD OR CREASE THE FINGERPRINT CHART.

(3) **Biographic Information.**—Complete every item in the Biographic Information form furnished you with this application and sign your name on the line provided. If you have ever served in the Armed Forces of the United States, obtain and complete also an extra yellow sheet of the form, bearing the number G-325B.

(4) **U.S. Military Service.**—If your application is based on your military service, obtain and complete Form N—426, "Request for Certification of Military or Naval Service."

2. **FEE.**—DO NOT SEND any fee with this application unless you are also applying for a certificate of citizenship for a child (see Instruction 6).

3. **ALIEN REGISTRATION RECEIPT CARD.**—DO NOT SEND your Alien Registration Receipt Card with this application.

4. **EXAMINATION ON GOVERNMENT AND LITERACY.**—Every person applying for naturalization must show that he or she has a knowledge and understanding of the history, principles, and form of government of the United States. THERE IS NO EXEMPTION FROM THIS REQUIREMENT, and you will therefore be examined on these subjects when you appear before the examiner with your witnesses.

You will also be examined on your ability to read, write and speak English. If on the date of your examination you are more than 50 years of age and have been a lawful permanent resident of the United States for 20 or more years, you will be exempt from the English language requirements of the law. If you are exempt, you may take the examination in any language you wish.

5. **OATH OF ALLEGIANCE.**—You will be required to take the following oath of allegiance to the United States in order to become a citizen:

I hereby declare, on oath, that I absolutely and entirely renounce and abjure all allegiance and fidelity to any foreign prince, potentate, state or sovereignty, of whom or which I have heretofore been a subject or citizen; that I will support and defend the Constitution and laws of the United States of America against all enemies, foreign and domestic; that I will bear true faith and allegiance to the same; that I will bear arms on behalf of the United States when required by the law; that I will perform noncombatant service in the armed forces of the United States when required by the law; that I will perform work of national importance under civilian direction when required by the law; and that I take this obligation freely without any mental reservation or purpose of evasion; so help me God.

If you cannot promise to bear arms or perform noncombatant service because of religious training and belief, you may omit those promises when taking the oath.

"Religious training and belief" means a person's belief in a relation to a Supreme Being involving duties superior to those arising from any human relation, but does not include essentially political, sociological, or philosophical views or a merely personal moral code.

---

6. THIS BLOCK APPLIES ONLY TO APPLICANTS WHO HAVE FOREIGN-BORN CHILDREN WHO ARE UNDER 18 YEARS OF AGE.

Some or all of your *own* foreign-born children (Not Step-Children) who are not yet citizens may possibly become United States citizens automatically when you are naturalized. This will happen:

(1) If the child is a lawful permanent resident of the United States and still under 18 years of age when you are naturalized, and

(2) The child's other parent is already a citizen or becomes a citizen before or at the same time that you become naturalized. If, however, the child's other parent is deceased, or if you are divorced and have custody of the child, then it makes no difference that the child's other parent was or is an alien.

(3) If your child is illegitimate and you are the mother, only (1) above applies.

(4) If the child is adopted, and was adopted before its 16th birthday and is in your custody.

If you wish, you can apply for a Certificate of Citizenship for any of these children, which will show that they are United States citizens. If you do not want such a Certificate, write "DO NOT" in Question (34), page 3; if you do want such a Certificate, write "DO" in Question (34), page 3, and send the following with this application:

(1) Fee. Fifteen dollars ($15) for **each** child for whom a certificate is desired. DO NOT SEND CASH IN THE MAIL. ALL FEES MUST BE SUBMITTED IN THE EXACT AMOUNT. If you mail your application, attach a money order or check, payable to *Immigration and Naturalization Service, Department of Justice*. (Exceptions: If you reside in the Virgin Islands, remittance must be payable to Commissioner of Finance, Virgin Islands; and if in Guam, to Treasurer, Guam). Personal checks are accepted subject to collectibility. An uncollectible check will render the application and any documents issued pursuant thereto invalid. A charge of $5.00 will be imposed if a check in payment of a fee is not honored by the bank on which it is drawn. The fee will be refunded if for any reason you are not naturalized in time or the child does not qualify for the certificate.

(2) Personal Description Form.—A completed Form N—604 for each child.

(3) Documents.—The documents applicable to your case listed in the blocks below. If you want any of the original documents returned to you, and if the law does not prohibit the making of copies, a photocopy of the document should be sent with the original document.

Any document in a foreign language must be accompanied by a summary translation in English. A summary translation is a condensation or abstract of the document's text. The translator must certify that he is competent to translate and that the translation is accurate.

(4) Photographs.—Follow Instruction No. 1 (1) and send three (3) photographs of each child. Write the child's Alien Registration Number on the back of the photographs, lightly in pencil.

DOCUMENTS REQUIRED WITH THIS APPLICATION

1. Child's birth certificate.
2. Your marriage certificate to child's other parent.
3. If you or the other parent were married before the marriage to each other, death certificate or divorce decree showing the termination of any previous marriage of each parent.
4. If the other parent became a citizen at birth, birth certificate of other parent.
5. If the child's other parent is deceased, or if you are divorced from the child's other parent, the death certificate or the divorce decree.
6. If the child is adopted, adoption decree.

SECONDARY EVIDENCE

If it is not possible to obtain any one of the required documents shown in the block above, consideration may be given to the following documents. In such case you must present a written explanation as to why the document listed in the block above is not being presented, together with a statement from the official custodian of the record showing that the document is not available.

1. *Baptismal certificate.*—A certificate under the seal of the church where the baptism occurred, showing date and place of child's birth, date of baptism, the names of the child's parents, and names of the godparents, if shown.

2. *School record.*—A letter from the school authorities having jurisdiction over the school attended (preferably the first school), showing date of admission to the school, child's date of birth or age at that time, place of birth, and the names and places of birth of parents, if shown in the school records.

3. If you or the other parent were married before the marriage to each other, death certificate or divorce decree showing the termination of any person(s) listed.

4. *Affidavits.*—Notarized affidavits of two persons who were living at the time, and who have personal knowledge of the event you are trying to prove—for example, the date and place of a birth, marriage, or death. The persons making the affidavits may be relatives and need not be citizens of the United States. Each affidavit should contain the following information regarding the person making the affidavit; His (Her) full name and address; date and place of birth; relationship to you, if any; full information concerning the event; and complete details concerning how he (she) acquired knowledge of the event.

APPLICATION TO FILE PETITION FOR NATURALIZATION

Mail or take to:

IMMIGRATION AND NATURALIZATION SERVICE

(See INSTRUCTIONS. BE SURE YOU UNDERSTAND EACH QUESTION BEFORE YOU ANSWER IT. PLEASE PRINT OR TYPE.)

FEE STAMP

ALIEN REGISTRATION
(Show the exact spelling of your name as it appears on your alien registration receipt card, and the number of your card. If you did not register, so state.)
Name ....
No. ....

Section of Law .... (Leave Blank)

Date: ....

(1) My full true and correct name is... (Full true name without abbreviations)

(2) I now live at... (Number and street,)

.... (City - county, state, zip code)

(3) I was born on........................ in...
(Month) (Day) (Year)   (City or town)   (County, province, or state)   (Country)

(4) I request that my name be changed to...

(5) Other names I have used are: .... (Include maiden name)   Sex: ☐ Male   ☐ Female

(6) Was your father or mother ever a United States citizen?.. ☐ Yes ☐ No
(If "Yes", explain fully)

(7) Can you read and write English?.. ☐ Yes ☐ No

(8) Can you speak English?.. ☐ Yes ☐ No

(9) Can you sign your name in English?.. ☐ Yes ☐ No

(10) My lawful admission for permanent residence was on..under the name of
(Month) (Day) (Year)

.... at...................
(City) (State)

(11) Since that date I have resided continuously in the United States and continuously in the State of........................ where I now live since........................ During the last five years I have been physically present in the United States for a total of..........months.

(12) Do you intend to reside permanently in the United States? ☐ Yes ☐ No If "No," explain:

(13) In what places in the United States have you lived during the last 5 years? List present address FIRST.

From -	To -	STREET ADDRESS	CITY AND STATE
(a) ...., 19......	PRESENT TIME		
(b) ...., 19......	.........., 19......		
(c) ...., 19......	.........., 19......		
(d) ...., 19......	.........., 19......		

(14) (a) Have you been out of the United States since your lawful admission as a permanent resident?....................... ☐ Yes ☐ No
If "Yes" fill in the following information for every absence of *less than 6 months*, no matter how short it was.

DATE DEPARTED	DATE RETURNED	NAME OF SHIP, OR OF AIRLINE, RAILROAD COMPANY, BUS COMPANY, OR OTHER MEANS USED TO RETURN TO THE UNITED STATES	PLACE OR PORT OF ENTRY THROUGH WHICH YOU RETURNED TO THE UNITED STATES

(b) Since your lawful admission, have you been out of the United States for a period of *6 months or longer?*.......... ☐ Yes ☐ No
If "No", state "None"; If "Yes", fill in following information for every absence of more than 6 months.

DATE DEPARTED	DATE RETURNED	NAME OF SHIP OR OF AIRLINE, RAILROAD COMPANY, BUS COMPANY, OR OTHER MEANS USED TO RETURN TO THE UNITED STATES	PLACE OR PORT OF ENTRY THROUGH WHICH YOU RETURNED TO THE UNITED STATES

(15) The law provides that you may not be regarded as qualified for naturalization, if you knowingly committed certain offenses or crimes, even though you may not have been arrested. Have you ever, in or outside the United States:

    (a) knowingly committed any crime for which you have not been arrested? .... ☐ Yes ☐ No

    (b) been arrested, cited, charged, indicted, convicted, fined or imprisoned for breaking or violating any law or ordinance, including traffic regulations? .... ☐ Yes ☐ No

If you answer "Yes" to (a) or (b), give the following information as to each incident.

	WHEN	WHERE	(City)	(State)	(Country)	NATURE OF OFFENSE	OUTCOME OF CASE, IF ANY
(a)							
(b)							
(c)							
(d)							
(e)							

(16) List your present and past membership in or affiliation with every organization, association, fund, foundation, party, club, society or similar group in the United States or in any other country or place, and your foreign military service. (If none, write "None.")

(a)		, 19........	to 19........
(b)		, 19........	to 19........
(c)		, 19........	to 19........
(d)		, 19........	to 19........
(e)		, 19........	to 19........
(f)		, 19........	to 19........
(g)		, 19........	to 19........

(17) (a) Are you now, or have you ever, in the United States or in any other place, been a member of, or in any other way connected or associated with the Communist Party? (If "Yes", attach full explanation) .... ☐ Yes ☐ No

    (b) Have you ever knowingly aided or supported the Communist Party directly, or indirectly through another organization, group or person? (If "Yes", attach full explanation) .... ☐ Yes ☐ No

    (c) Do you now or have you ever advocated, taught, believed in, or knowingly supported or furthered the interests of Communism? (If "Yes", attach full explanation) .... ☐ Yes ☐ No

(18) Have you borne any hereditary title or have you ever been of any order of nobility in any foreign state? .... ☐ Yes ☐ No

(19) **Have you ever been declared legally incompetent or have you ever been confined as a patient in a mental institution?** ········· ☐ Yes ☐ No

(20) Are deportation proceedings pending against you, or have you ever been deported or ordered deported, or have you ever applied for suspension of deportation? .... ☐ Yes ☐ No

(21) (a) My last Federal income tax return was filed............................ (year) Do you owe any Federal taxes? .... ☐ Yes ☐ No

    (b) Since becoming a permanent resident of the United States, have you:

    —filed an income tax return as a nonresident? .... ☐ Yes ☐ No

    —failed to file an income tax return because you regarded yourself as a nonresident? .... ☐ Yes ☐ No

    (If you answer "Yes" to (a) or (b) explain fully.)

(22) Have you ever claimed in writing, or in any other way, to be a United States citizen? .... ☐ Yes ☐ No

(23) (a) Have you ever deserted from the military, air, or naval forces of the United States? .... ☐ Yes ☐ No

    (b) If male, have you ever left the United States to avoid being drafted into the Armed Forces of the United States? ...... ☐ Yes ☐ No

(24) The law provides that you may not be regarded as qualified for naturalization if, at *any* time during the period for which you are required to prove good moral character, you have been a habitual drunkard; committed adultery; advocated or practiced polygamy; have been a prostitute or procured anyone for prostitution; have knowingly and for gain helped any alien to enter the United States illegally; have been an illicit trafficker in narcotic drugs or marijuana; have received your income mostly from illegal gambling, or have given false testimony for the purpose of obtaining any benefits under this Act. Have you ever, *anywhere*, been such a person or committed any of these acts? (If you answer yes to any of these, attach full explanation.) .... ☐ Yes ☐ No

(25) Do you believe in the Constitution and form of government of the United States? .... ☐ Yes ☐ No

(26) Are you willing to take the full oath of allegiance to the United States? (See Instructions) .... ☐ Yes ☐ No

(27) If the law requires it, are you willing:

    (a) to bear arms on behalf of the United States? (If "No", attach full explanation) .... ☐ Yes ☐ No

    (b) to perform noncombatant services in the Armed Forces of the United States? (If "No", attach full explanation) ···· ☐ Yes ☐ No

    (c) to perform work of national importance under civilian direction? (If "No"', attach full explanation) .... ☐ Yes ☐ No

(28) (a) If male, did you ever register under United States Selective Service laws or draft laws? .... ☐ Yes ☐ No

    If "Yes" give date....................; Selective Service No.......................; Local Board No.....................; Present classification....................

    (b) Did you ever apply for exemption from military service because of alienage, conscientious objections, or other reasons? ☐ Yes ☐ No

    If "Yes," explain fully..

(29) If serving or ever served in the Armed Forces of the United States, give branch...;

from.........................., 19........ to ...., 19......., and from.........................., 19...... to ...., 19......;

☐ inducted or ☐ enlisted at...; Service No.................................;

type of discharge..; ....; rank at discharge.......................................;

    (Honorable, Dishonorable, etc.)

reason for discharge...

    (alienage, conscientious objector, other)

☐ Reserve or ☐ National Guard from.. 19........ to..............................

(30) My occupation is...

List the names, addresses, and occupations (or types of business) of your employers during the last 5 years?   (If none, write "None.")
List present employment FIRST.

FROM-	TO-	EMPLOYER'S NAME	ADDRESS	OCCUPATION OR TYPE OF BUSINESS
(a) ...., 19......	.......PRESENT TIME			
(b) ...., 19......	................., 19......			
(c) ...., 19......	................., 19......			
(d) ...., 19......	................., 19......			

(31) Complete this block if you are or have been married.

I am.. The first name of my husband or wife is (was)...............................
    (Single, married, divorced, widowed)

We were married on........................... at... He or she was born at...................................

.... on........................... He or she entered the United States at (place).............................

.... on (date)........................... for permanent residence and now resides ☐ with me

☐ apart from me at ....
    (Show full address if not living with you.)

He or she was naturalized on........................... at...; Certificate No...........................,

or became a citizen by .... His or her alien Registration No. is...........................

(32) How many times have you been married?............ How many times has your husband or wife been married?............ If either of you has
been married more than once, fill in the following information for each previous marriage.

DATE MARRIED	DATE MARRIAGE ENDED	NAME OF PERSON TO WHOM MARRIED	SEX	(Check One) PERSON MARRIED WAS CITIZEN ☐ ALIEN ☐	HOW MARRIAGE ENDED
(a)				☐ .... ☐	
(b)				☐ .... ☐	
(c)				☐ .... ☐	
(d)				☐ .... ☐	

(33) I have................children: (Complete columns (a) to (h) as to each child. If child lives with you, state "with me" in column (h), other-
    (Number)   wise give city and State of child's residence.)

(a) Given Names	(b) Sex	(c) Place Born (Country)	(d) Date Born	(e) Date of Entry	(f) Port of Entry	(g) Alien Registration No.	(h) Now Living at-

(34) **READ INSTRUCTION NO. 6 BEFORE ANSWERING QUESTION (36)**

I..................................want certificates of citizenship for those of my children who are in the U.S. and are under age 18 years that are named below.
   (Do)   (Do Not)

(Enclose $15 for each child for whom you want certificates, otherwise, send no money with this application.)

....
                (Write names of children under age 18 years and who are in the U.S. for whom you want certificates)

If present spouse is not the parent of the children named above, give parent's name, date and place of naturalization, and number of marriages

....

Signature of person preparing form, if other than applicant.	SIGNATURE OF APPLICANT
I declare that this document was prepared by me at the request of applicant and is based on all information of which I have any knowledge. SIGNATURE	ADDRESS AT WHICH APPLICANT RECEIVES MAIL
ADDRESS: DATE:	
	APPLICANT'S TELEPHONE NUMBER

TO APPLICANT: DO NOT FILL IN BLANKS BELOW THIS LINE.

NOTE CAREFULLY.—This application must be sworn to before an officer of the Immigration and Naturalization Service at the time you appear before such officer for examination on this application.

AFFIDAVIT

I do swear that I know the contents of this application comprising pages 1 to 4, inclusive, and the supplemental forms thereto, No(s). ...., subscribed to by me; that the same are true to the best of my knowledge and belief; that corrections numbered ( ) to ( ) were made by me or at my request; and that this application was signed by me with my full, true, and correct name, SO HELP ME GOD.

Subscribed and sworn to before me by applicant at the preliminary investigation ( ) at ....

....

this .... day of ...., 19.......

I certify that before verification the above applicant stated in my presence that he/she had (heard) read the foregoing application, corrections therein and supplemental form(s) and understood the contents thereof.

....
(Complete and true signature of applicant)

....
(Naturalization examiner)

(For demonstration of applicant's ability to write English)

(1st witness. Occupation) ....

(2nd witness. Occupation) ....

Nonfiled ....

....
(Date, Reasons)

NOTICE TO APPLICANTS:

Authority for collection of the information requested on this form and those forms mentioned in the instructions thereto is continued in Sections 328, 329, 332, 334, 335 or 341 of the Immigration and Nationality Act of 1952 (8 U.S.C. 1439, 1440, 1443, 1445, 1446 or 1452). Submission of the information is voluntary inasmuch as the immigration and nationality laws of the United States do not require an alien to apply for naturalization. If your Social Security number is included on a form, no right, benefit or privilege will be denied for your failure to provide such number. However, as military records are indexed by such numbers, verification of your military service, if required to establish eligibility for naturalization, may prove difficult. The principal purposes for soliciting the information are to enable designated officers of the Immigration and Naturalization Service to determine the admissibility of a petitioner for naturalization and to make appropriate recommendations to the naturalization courts. All or any part of the information solicited may, as a matter of routine use, be disclosed to a court exercising naturalization jurisdiction and to other federal, state, local or foreign law enforcement or regulatory agencies, Department of Defense, including any component thereof, the Selective Service System, the Department of State, the Department of the Treasury, Central Intelligence Agency, Interpol and individuals and organizations in the processing of the application or petition for naturalization, or during the course of investigation to elicit further information required by the Immigration and Naturalization Service to carry out its function. Information solicited which indicates a violation or potential violation of law, whether civil, criminal or regulatory in nature may be referred, as routine use, to the appropriate agency, whether federal, state, local or foreign, charged with the responsibility of investigating, enforcing or prosecuting such violations. Failure to provide any or all of the solicited information may result in an adverse recommendation to the court as to an alien's eligibility for naturalization and denial by the court of a petition for naturalization.

For sale by the Superintendent of Documents, U.S. Government Printing Office
Washington, D.C. 20402 (per 100)
Stock Number 027-002-00282-6

☆ U.S. GOVERNMENT PRINTING OFFICE: 1980-306-781